WRITER–FILES

General Editor: Simon Trussler

Associate Editor: Malcolm Page

File on
OSBORNE

Compiled by Malcolm Page

Methuen. London and New York

A Methuen Paperback
First published in 1988 as a paperback original
by Methuen London Ltd,
11 New Fetter Lane, London EC4P 4EE
and Methuen Inc, 29 West 35th Street,
New York, NY 10001

Copyright in the compilation
©1988 by Malcolm Page
Copyright in the series format
©1988 by Methuen London Ltd
Copyright in the editorial presentation
©1988 by Simon Trussler

Typeset in 9/10 Times
by L.Anderson Typesetting,
Woodchurch, Kent, TN26 3TB

Printed in Great Britain by
Richard Clay Ltd,
Bungay, Suffolk.

British Library Cataloguing in Publication Data

Page, Malcolm
    File on Osborne. – (Writer-files)
    1. Osborne, John, *1929* – Criticism and interpretation
    I. Title   II. Series
    822'.914   PR6029.S39

    ISBN 0-413-14460-7

Contents

General Editor's Introduction 5

1: A Brief Chronology 7

2: The Plays
The Devil Inside 10
Personal Enemy 11
Look Back in Anger 11
The Entertainer 17
Epitaph for George Dillon 21
The World of Paul Slickey 24
A Subject of Scandal and Concern 26
Luther 27
The Blood of the Bambergs 33
Under Plain Cover 34
Tom Jones 36
Inadmissible Evidence 37
A Patriot for Me 43
A Bond Honoured 49
Time Present 52
The Hotel in Amsterdam 55
The Right Prospectus 59
West of Suez 60
Hedda Gabler 65
A Sense of Detachment 66
A Place Calling Itself Rome 68
Ms., or Jill and Jack 69
The Gift of Friendship 70
The End of Me Old Cigar 72
The Picture of Dorian Gray 74
Watch It Come Down 76
Almost a Vision 78
Try a Little Tenderness 79
You're Not Watching Me, Mummy 79
Very Like a Whale 80
God Rot Tunbridge Wells 81

3: Non-Dramatic Writing 82

4: The Writer on His Work 84

5: A Select Bibliography 86
 a. Primary Sources 86
 b. Secondary Sources 89

The theatre is, by its nature, an ephemeral art: yet it is a daunting task to track down the newspaper reviews, or contemporary statements from the writer or his director, which are often all that remain to help us recreate some sense of what a particular production was like. This series is therefore intended to make readily available a selection of the comments that the critics made about the plays of leading modern dramatists at the time of their production — and to trace, too, the course of each writer's own views about his work and his world.

In addition to combining a uniquely convenient source of such elusive *documentation*, the 'Writer–Files' series also assembles the *information* necessary for readers to pursue further their interest in a particular writer or work. Variations in quantity between one writer's output and another, differences in temperament which make some readier than others to talk about their work, and the variety of critical response, all mean that the presentation and balance of material shifts between one volume and another: but we have tried to arrive at a format for the series which will nevertheless enable users of one volume readily to find their way around any other.

Section 1, 'A Brief Chronology', provides a quick conspective overview of each playwright's life and his career. *Section 2* deals with the plays themselves, arranged chronologically in the order of their composition: information on first performances, major revivals, and publication is followed by a brief synopsis (for quick reference set in slightly larger, italic type), then by a representative selection of the critical response, and of the dramatist's own comments on the play and its theme.

Section 3 offers concise guidance to each writer's work in non-dramatic forms, while *Section 4*, 'The Writer on His Work', brings together comments from the playwright himself on more general matters of construction, opinion, and artistic development. Finally, *Section 5* provides a bibliographical guide to other primary and secondary sources of further reading, among which full details will be found of works cited elsewhere under short titles, and of collected editions of the plays — but not of individual titles, particulars of which will be found with the other factual data in Section 2.

The 'Writer-Files' hope by striking this kind of balance between information and a wide range of opinion to offer 'companions' to the study of major playwrights in the modern repertoire — not in that dangerous pre-digested fashion which can too readily quench the desire to read the plays themselves,

General Editor's Introduction

nor so prescriptively as to allow any single line of approach to predominate, but rather to encourage readers to form their own judgements of the plays in a wide-ranging context of contrasting opinions.

John Osborne wrote *Look Back in Anger* in 1956, the year of the Suez crisis and the Soviet suppression of the Hungarian revolution — and his last major work, *Hotel in Amsterdam*, in 1968, the year of the tragically brief 'Prague spring', of student rebellion in the streets of Paris, and of violence on American campuses against the war in Vietnam. Between those major political and social watersheds, a whole generation in England had had to come to terms with the end of the lingering imperial dream — a process to which Osborne's plays contributed valuable if often tangential insights. But the 'sense of detachment', echoed in the title of a later play, seemed to prevent Osborne from any reconcilement with the new England whose values he had, ironically, helped to shape: and my own generation of theatregoers felt no less betrayed by his seeming desertion of our cause than he did by the flabbiness of the permissive society and all its works.

So a younger group of theatre critics found itself unhappy about Osborne's new work, just as their predecessors had been outraged by his earlier plays. The consequence, as reflected in this volume, is the critical hostility which has always dogged him, tempered to querulous complaints about flawed structure or muddled themes at the peak of his success, but at the beginning as wary of the upstart young pup as of the reactionary old fogey later on. I hasten to add that I use both terms ironically, and that one of the values of the present volume is that it enables the student to trace the threads of consistency in Osborne's outlook and approach, hidden though these have often been by the particularities of his own or his critics' rhetoric.

One continues to hope for the 'great work' of Osborne's middle years: not necessarily one which will again 'speak for a generation', new or old, but which will speak for *himself* as the best of his earlier work did with a flawless if instinctive fusion of form and substance. Arguably, he has already written it, but in the quite different form of autobiography — for his old champions, a lonelier and less challenging art than the theatre.

Simon Trussler

1929 12 Dec., born in Fulham, son of commercial artist and copywriter, and Nellie Beatrice, a barmaid.

1936 Family moved to Stoneleigh, Surrey.

1938 Family moved to Ewell.

1941 Death of father.

1942 Sick for a year with rheumatic fever.

1943 To a boarding school in Devon, St. Michael's. 'St. Michael's was probably not much seedier or inefficient than many other schools of its kind, offering the merest, timid trappings of a fake public school for the minimum expense' (*A Better Class of Person,* p. 128).

1945 Summer, expelled for hitting a teacher.

1947 Works as junior journalist on trade papers, *Gas World, Nursery World* , and *The Miller.*

1948 Enters theatre as Assistant Stage Manager on 48-week tour of *No Room at the Inn*; on stage as understudy.

1950 Acting with companies in Ilfracombe, the London area, and Hayling Island, where he played Hamlet: 'It was a passable impersonation of Claudius after a night's carousing' (*A Better Class of Person,* p. 233). Co-author of *The Devil Inside,* staged Huddersfield.

1951 Acting in Bridgwater; marries Pamela Lane there.

1952-54 Acting in Kidderminster; tour of South Wales in *Pygmalion.*

1955 Co-author of *Personal Enemy,* staged Harrogate.

1956 May, actor with English Stage Co. at Royal Court Theatre, London, as Antonio in *Don Juan* and Lionel in *The Death of Satan* (double-bill by Ronald Duncan). June, three parts in *Cards of Identity.* Oct., Lin To in *The Good Woman of Setzuan. Look Back in Anger* a success at Royal Court.

1957 *The Entertainer* staged. Divorced Pamela Lane and married Mary Ure, who acted in *Look Back in Anger.* Played Commissionaire in *Apollo de Bellac* and Donald Blake in *The Making of Moo* at the Royal Court.

1958 *Epitaph for George Dillon* (written earlier with Anthony Creighton) staged. Bought houses in Chelsea and, with 23-acre estate, at Edenbridge, Kent, where he still lives.

1959 *The World of Paul Slickey*, directed by Osborne, staged.

1960 *A Subject of Scandal and Concern* televised.

1961 *Luther* staged. Member of Committee of 100, for unilateral nuclear disarmament through civil disobedience; arrested in Trafalgar Square sit-down and fined.

1962 *Plays for England*, double-bill, staged.

1963 Divorced Mary Ure and married Penelope Gilliatt, novelist and journalist. Wrote script for successful film, *Tom Jones*, and in these years wrote scripts for three films not made: *The Hostage, The Secret Agent,* and *Moll Flanders*.

1964 *Inadmissible Evidence* staged. Played Claude Hickett in *A Cuckoo in the Nest* at Royal Court.

1965 *A Patriot for Me* staged. Directed *Meals on Wheels*, by Charles Wood, at Royal Court.

1966 *A Bond Honoured* staged at the National Theatre.

1967 Divorced Penelope Gilliatt; they had one daughter.

1968 Married Jill Bennett, an actress. *Time Present* and *The Hotel in Amsterdam* staged. Acted in *The Parachute*, by David Mercer, on TV. Work on film-script of *The Charge of the Light Brigade*, with Charles Wood.

1969 Acted in *The First Night of Pygmalion* on TV and as Maidanov in *First Love*, a film.

1970 *The Right Prospectus* televised. Acted in *Get Carter*, a film.

1971 *West of Suez* staged.

1972 *Hedda Gabler*, an adaptation from Ibsen, and *A Sense of Detachment* staged.

1973 *Jill and Jack* and *A Gift of Friendship* televised. Directed his *The Entertainer* at Greenwich Theatre.

1975 *The End of Me Old Cigar* and *The Picture of Dorian Gray* staged.

1976 *Watch It Come Down* staged at National Theatre. *Almost a Vision* televised.

1977 Divorced Jill Bennett. Acted in *Lady Charlotte* on TV.

1978 Married Helen Dawson, drama critic. Acted in *Tomorrow Never Comes*, a film. Directed his *Inadmissible Evidence* at Royal Court.

1980   *You're Not Watching Me, Mummy* and *Very Like a Whale* .

1981   *A Better Class of Person*, autobiography, published.

1982   Television critic of *Mail on Sunday*, for three months.

1985   *A Better Class of Person* and *God Rot Tunbridge Wells* televised.

The Devil Inside

A play, co-authored with Stella Linden.
First production: Huddersfield, May 1950.
Unpublished.

A strange melodrama about a Welsh youth whom the villagers think an idiot and his relations a sex-maniac because he writes poetry; his talents are recognized by a visiting medical student, but meanwhile he is constrained to kill a local girl who attacks his idea of beauty by attempting to pass him off as the father of her child.

John Russell Taylor, *Anger and After*
(London, revised ed., 1969), p. 39-40

In the dressing-room at the Empire, Sunderland, I began writing my first play, a melodrama about a poetic Welsh loon called *Resting Deep*. It had nothing to do with my own experience and certainly none of what might be occasionally found in the drab world of George Dillon. . . . If I was willing to sit down with Stella and start to rework the play from scratch [Stella and her husband] would be prepared to include it in a new season which they projected. Was I willing to agree? I most certainly was. . . . Stella and I had finished work on *Resting Deep*, which had now been retitled *The Devil Inside*. Stella had given it a Pinero uplift and added a few coarse jokes, one of which I remember was someone coming on and singing a song called, 'I love to play with your snowballs. There are no balls like your snowballs.' How this got past the Lord Chamberlain at the time is a mystery. . . . On Easter [?Whit] Monday 1950 I sat in the stalls of the Theatre Royal, Huddersfield, watching the world opening performance of my play, holding hands with my co-author. . . . Stella's coarse jokes worked, as she said they would, but my remaining wastegrounds of poetry palled even for me. . . . My share of the royalty was just over nine pounds.

Osborne, *A Better Class of Person*,
p. 185, 196, 202, 220

Personal Enemy

A play, co-written with Anthony Creighton.
First production: Harrogate, 1 Mar. 1955.
Unpublished.

It was the summer of 1954. Work was hard to come by. The McCarthy trials were at their height and I drove myself to some interest in them. . . . I spent several weeks in the American Library in Grosvenor Square, reading transcripts of the Un-American Activities Committee, taking them back home and going over them with Anthony. Out of laziness or want of companionship I agreed to write a play with him based on his own melodramatic plot. Perhaps I felt that with my writing and editing of the transcript it could be turned into a superior kind of Patrick Desmond package, specious liberalism sentimentalized.

Osborne, *A Better Class of Person*, p. 255

Look Back in Anger

A play in three acts.
First production: Royal Court Th., 8 May 1956
    (dir. Tony Richardson; with Kenneth Haigh as Jimmy Porter,
    Mary Ure as Alison, Alan Bates as Cliff, Helena Hughes as Helena,
    and John Welsh as Colonel Redfern), transferred to Lyric Th.,
    Hammersmith, 5 Nov. 1956 with Richard Pasco as Jimmy,
    Doreen Aris as Alison, Vivienne Drummond as Helena, and
    Kenneth Edwards as Colonel Redfern), transferred back to
    Royal Court Th., 11 Mar. 1957 (with Heather Sears as Alison and
    Deering Wells as Colonel Redfern).
Revivals: Royal Court Th., 28 Oct. 1957 (dir. John Dexter; with
    Alec McCowen as Jimmy and Clare Austin as Alison). Royal Court
    Th., 29 Oct. 1968 (dir. Anthony Page; with Victor Henry as Jimmy,
    Jane Asher as Alison, and Martin Shaw as Cliff).
First New York production: 1 Oct. 1957 (dir. Tony Richardson, with
    Kenneth Haigh as Jimmy, Mary Ure as Alison, and Alan Bates
    as Cliff).
New York revival: Roundabout Th., 19 June 1980 (dir. Ted Craig; with
    Malcolm McDowell as Jimmy).
Film: script by Osborne and Nigel Kneale, 1959 (dir. Tony Richardson;

with Richard Burton as Jimmy, Mary Ure as Alison, Claire Bloom as Helena, and and Gary Redmond as Cliff).

Published: Faber, 1957.

Jimmy Porter is an articulate, discontented graduate of a 'White Tile' university, a jazz-lover, running a sweet stall in a Midlands town. He is perpetually angry, lamenting that 'there aren't any good, brave causes left.' He is seen in his squalid flat, bored, with the papers, which he divides into 'posh' and 'wet,' on a Sunday evening, grumbling at the noise of church bells. His usual target is Alison, his upper-class wife, wearily ironing; their lodger is Cliff, an easy-going Welsh youth. Helena, an actress and friend of Alison's, comes to stay. She persuades Alison to leave and Colonel Redfern, Alison's father, comes for her. Helena takes Alison's place in the flat till Alison returns, having had a miscarriage. Jimmy and Alison re-unite, playing a childish game of bears and squirrels.

Jimmy Porter is a young man who is anxious to give a great deal, and is hurt because no-one seems interested enough to take it—including his wife.

> Osborne, Introduction to Samuel French ed. of play

It's not the usual drawing room comedy—but the people recognized it as something real, something that was happening to them. . . . Jimmy Porter isn't unpleasant, really; he is careful, good humoured and honest, although he may be wrongheaded sometimes. He belongs to a class that wants to keep its identity.

> Osborne, quoted by David Dempsey, 'Most Angry Fella',
> *New York Times Magazine,* 20 Oct. 1957, p. 22, 27

I thought *Look Back in Anger* was a formal, rather old-fashioned play, I think that it broke out by its use of language.

> Osborne, 'That Awful Museum', *Twentieth Century,*
> 169, Feb. 1961, p. 214

I thought *Look Back in Anger* was quite a comedy. But nobody else did. They thought it was a 'Human Drama.'

> Osborne, quoted by Mark Amory, 'Jester Flees the Court',
> *Sunday Times Magazine,* 24 Nov. 1974, p. 34

John Osborne didn't contribute to the British theatre: he set off a land-mine called *Look Back in Anger* and blew most of it up. The bits have settled back into place, of course, but it can never be the same again.

Alan Sillitoe, *Look Back in Anger: a Casebook*, p. 185

8 May 1956 still marks the real breakthrough of 'the new drama' into the British theatre, and Osborne himself remains . . . the first of the angry young men and arguably the biggest shock to the system of British theatre since the advent of Shaw.

John Russell Taylor, *Anger and After* (revised ed., 1969), p. 39

Look Back in Anger presents post-war youth as it really is, with special emphasis on the non-U intelligentsia who live in bed-sitters and divide the Sunday papers into two groups, 'posh' and 'wet.' To have done this at all would be a signal achievement; to have done it in a first play is a minor miracle. All the qualities are there, qualities one had despaired of ever seeing on the stage—the drift towards anarchy, the instinctive left-ishness, the automatic rejection of 'official' attitudes, the surrealist sense of humour (Jimmy describes a pansy friend as 'a female Emily Bronte'), the casual promiscuity, the sense of lacking a crusade worth fighting for and, underlying all these, the determination that no-one who dies shall go unmourned.

One cannot imagine Jimmy Porter listening with a straight face to speeches about our inalienable right to flog Cypriot schoolboys. You could never mobilize him and his kind into a lynching mob, since the art he lives for, jazz, was invented by Negroes; and if you gave him a razor, he would do nothing with it but shave. The Porters of our time deplore the tyranny of 'good taste' and refuse to accept 'emotional' as a term of abuse; they are classless, and they are also leaderless. Mr. Osborne is their first spokesman in the London theatre. . . .

It is twenty minutes too long, and not even Mr. Haigh's bravura could blind me to the painful whimsey of the final reconciliation scene. I agree that *Look Back in Anger* is likely to remain a minority taste. What matters, however, is the size of the minority. I estimate it at roughly 6,733,000, which is the number of people in this country between the ages of twenty and thirty. And this figure will doubtless be swelled by refugees from other age-groups who are curious to know precisely what the contemporary young pup is thinking and feeling. I doubt if I could love anyone who did not wish to see *Look Back in Anger*. It is the best young play of its decade.

Kenneth Tynan, *Look Back in Anger: a Casebook*, p. 49-51,
from *The Observer*, 13 May 1956

By putting the sex war and the class war on to one and the same stage, Mr. Osborne gave the drama a tremendous nudge forwards. Most of modern thought, outside the theatre, has been devoted to making Freud shake hands with Marx; within the theatre, they are mighty incompatibles. Social plays are traditionally sexless, and plays about sex are mostly non-social. Jimmy Porter is politically a liberal and sexually a despot. Whether we like him or not, we must concede that he is a character with a full set of attitudes, towards society as well as personal relations. Others may solve Jimmy's problem: Mr. Osborne is the first to state it. No germinal play of comparable strength has emerged since the war.

Kenneth Tynan, *The Observer*, 30 Dec. 1956

I wonder why it is that. . . .

Nobody has yet observed that, as a piece of dramatic construction, *Look Back in Anger* is *A Streetcar Named Desire* seen from Stanley Kowalski's point of view; or that there are marked resemblances between Archie Rice, the itinerant failure, 'living on a smile and a shoestring,' and Willie Loman in *Death of a Salesman*?

People who profess themselves disgusted by the self-pity of Archie in *The Entertainer* accept without a qualm such self-pitying foreigners as Oedipus, Hamlet, Phèdre and most of Chekhov's Russians?

Kenneth Tynan, 'Brief Chronicle', *The Observer*, 10 Nov. 1957, p. 19

Good taste, reticence and middle-class understatement were convicted of hypocrisy and jettisoned on the spot; replacing them, John Osborne spoke out in a vein of ebullient, free-wheeling rancour that betokened the arrival of something new in the theatre—a sophisticated, articulate lower-class. Most of the critics were offended by Jimmy Porter, but not on account of his anger; a working-class hero is expected to be angry. What nettled them was something quite different: his self-confidence. This was no envious inferior whose insecurity they could pity. Jimmy Porter talked with the wit and assurance of a young man who not only knew he was right but had long since mastered the vocabulary wherewith to express his knowledge. Osborne's success breached the dam, and there followed a cascade of plays about impoverished people. Such plays had existed before; the novelty lay in the fact that the emphasis was now on the people rather than on their poverty. For the first time it was possible for a character in English drama to be poor and intelligently amusing.

Kenneth Tynan, 'Look behind the Anger', *The Observer*, 27 Dec. 1959

In Anthony Page's production of *Look Back in Anger* Victor Henry stressed the pathos and neurotic isolation of Jimmy Porter: his Left-wing politics were a by-product of his neurosis. With Kenneth Haigh, the original Jimmy, it was the other way round: he was primarily a Socialist and only secondarily an emotional misfit. In retrospect, this jazz trumpeter from the white-tile university uncannily pre-figured two movements—student revolt and black militancy—that weren't to flower until the next decade: hence, no doubt, his frustration.

Kenneth Tynan, *The Observer*, 23 Feb. 1969

A good deal of Jimmy's railing falls into perspective as an attempt to goad his wife on more intimate, unspoken levels. The play no longer seems one man's battle against England. It appears as the struggle, equally anguished but wholly personal, within one marriage. . . . The use of Cliff, big-hearted and half-comprehending, as both battlefield and mediator between the warring pair, is subtly worked-out, a fine piece of dramatic geometry. The conflict of husband and wife is fierce and equal, as roundly theatrical as *Virginia Woolf*.

Ronald Bryden, *The Observer*, 3 Nov. 1968

The overwhelming impression now is one of rampant misogyny and pervasive sexism. Osborne came out as a misogynist in his recent autobiography, but such circumstantial evidence is redundant. You don't need to be a mathematical genius either to work out that when Jimmy Porter lambasts his mother, Alison's mother, Alison and Helena, they have one thing in common: they're not men. Only his friend Hugh Tanner's mother is exempt from vituperation. His fear of women is evident: Alison is described as sexually voracious, and Osborne was hardly innovative in his portrayal of female bitchiness, of woman supplanting woman. Alison is a cipher, struggling to view the world through Jimmy's eyes: no Nora, she leaves him and returns humbled. . . . Osborne gives us few clues that Porter ultimately should be considered anything but right. Michelene Wandor's *Understudies: Theatre and Sexual Politics* interestingly argues that it is not simply a misogynist play but one about the crisis of mid-20th century virility: Porter sublimates his sense of class hatred into sexual hatred and venomous attacks on women. . . . How political is *Look Back in Anger*? Is Jimmy Porter really a frustrated activist, a searcher after great causes? I suspect not. Would he now be a foot-sore marcher with a CND badge, would he have been there outside Grunwick? He is more likely to be a minor writer railing against publishers, or a minor publisher railing against writers.

Anne Karpf, 'Battle Stations', *The Listener*, 15 April 1982
(on a radio production)

On the film

The camera throws open the street door, children are running by; rain on the window prompts the umbrellas hurrying to church. In two very important particulars this going-about mends weaknesses in the play. One is that sweet-stall which at the Royal Court seemed no more than an odd, misjudged fancy: here in an all-alive-oh market, one is persuaded that —yes—in Jimmy Porter's martyrdom this may have been a phase. Then, hitherto a mere cursory mention, Ma Tanner (Edith Evans, beautifully subdued) walks and talks, lays flowers on a husband's grave, and is herself, finally, lowered in a coffin, so that she exists as something more than material for harangue. In other details, too, the ugliness of pensioners on a seat or cut-throat competition in the market, the film wins perspectives. . . . The harangues have been cut down, with epigrammatic effect, so that now more than ever Jimmy Porter looms as a Hamlet in low places, keeping the sting without the reiteration of opinion. The sense of something rotten in the state of Denmark Hill remains powerful, even if the Bishop and the H-bomb have gone and a fair whack of brother Nigel.

William Whitebait, *'Look Back in Anger'*,
New Statesman, 30 May 1959, p. 758

A selection of other articles and reviews

Clive Barker, *'Look Back in Anger:* the Turning Point', *Zeitschrift für Anglikstik und Amerikanistik*, 14, 1966, p. 367-71.

E.G. Bierhaus, Jr., ' "No World of its Own": *Look Back in Anger'*, *Modern Drama*, 19 (March 1976), p. 47-56.

John Ditsky, *The Onstage Christ* (London: Vision, 1980), p. 111-22.

A.E. Dyson, *'Look Back in Anger'*, *Critical Quarterly*, 1, 1959, p. 318-26; reprinted in *Modern British Dramatists*, ed. John Russell Brown (Englewood Cliffs, NJ, 1968).

David Edgar, 'The Diverse Progeny of Jimmy Porter', *New Society*, 6 Jan. 1983, p. 11-13.

John Elsom, ed., *Post-War British Theatre Criticism* (Routledge and Kegan Paul, 1981), p. 74-80.

Gareth and Barbara Lloyd Evans, eds., *Plays in Review, 1956-1980* (Batsford, 1985), p. 50-4.

J.H. Huizinga, *'Look Back* Looked Back on', *New Review*, No. 29, Aug. 1976, p. 59-62.

Roy Huss, 'John Osborne's Backward Half-Way Look', *Modern Drama*, 6, May 1963, p. 20-5.

John Kershaw, *The Present Stage* (Fontana, 1966), p. 21-42.

Brian Murphy, 'Jimmy Porter's Past: the Logic of Rage in *Look*

Back in Anger', *Midwest Quarterly*, 18, Summer 1977, p. 362-73.

Benedict Nightingale, *An Introduction to 50 Modern British Plays* (Pan, 1982), p. 292-305.

David Robinson, *'Look Back in Anger'*, *Sight and Sound*, 29, Nos. 3-4, Summer-Autumn 1959, p. 122-5, 179 [the film].

Patricia M. Spacks, 'Confrontation and Escape in Two Social Dramas', *Modern Drama*, May 1968, p. 61-72 [compared with *A Doll's House*].

Lois Spencer, *'Look Back in Anger'*, *Insight II: Analyses of Modern British Literature*, ed. John V. Hagopian and Martin Dolch (Frankfurt: Hirsch, 1970), p. 277-84.

John Russell Taylor, ed., *John Osborne: 'Look Back in Anger' : a Casebook* (London: Macmillan, 1968) [29 reviews, 8 'critical studies', various 'points of view', etc.].

Raymond Williams, *Drama from Ibsen to Brecht* (Chatto and Windus, 1968), p. 318-22.

The Entertainer

A play in three acts.

First production: Royal Court Th., London, 10 Apr. 1957 (dir. Tony Richardson; with Laurence Olivier as Archie Rice, Brenda de Banzie as Phoebe, George Relph as Billy Rice, Dorothy Tutin as Jean, Richard Pasco as Frank, and Stanley Meadows as Graham). Re-opened at the Palace Th., 10 Sept. 1957 (same cast, except Joan Plowright and later Geraldine McEwan as Jean, and Robert Stephens as Graham).

Revivals : in London: Greenwich Th., 28 Nov. 1974 (dir. John Osborne; with Max Wall as Archie Rice, Constance Chapman as Phoebe, Angela Pleasance as Jean, and Kenneth Cranham as Frank); Shaftesbury Th., 28 May 1986 (dir. Robin LeFevre; with Peter Bowles as Archie Rice, Sylvia Syms as Phoebe, and Frank Middlemass as Billy).

First New York production: Royale Th., 12 Feb. 1958 (dir. Tony Richardson; with Laurence Olivier as Archie Rice).

New York revival: Roundabout Th., 20 Jan. 1983 (dir. William Gaskill; with Nicol Williamson as Archie Rice and Frances Cuka as Phoebe).

Film: script by John Osborne and Nigel Kneale, 1960 (dir. Tony Richardson; with Laurence Olivier as Archie Rice, Brenda de Banzie as Phoebe, Joan Plowright as Jean, Roger Livesey as Billy Rice).

Published: Faber, 1957.

The life and times of Archie Rice, a third-rate music-hall comedian—who knows he is third-rate. His father, Billy, represents the Edwardian heyday of music-hall. The decline of music-hall is analogous to the decline of Britain ('Don't clap too hard, lady, It's a very old building'). Archie is thinking of divorcing his long-suffering wife, one son (Frank) is a conscientious objector while the other is held prisoner by the Egyptians: the time is of the British attack on Suez in October 1956. At the end of Act 2 they hear that he is dead. Archie's daughter, Jean, asks —'Is it really just for the sake of a gloved hand waving at you from a golden coach?' Billy dies, and Archie refuses the offer of his prosperous brother to send him to Canada. Jean asserts: 'We've only got ourselves. Somehow, we've just got to make a go of it.' Scenes alternate with song, dance and comic patter performances by Archie.

The music hall is dying, and, with it, a significant part of England. Some of the heart of England has gone; something that once belonged to everyone, for this was truly a folk art.

'Note', The Entertainer

I've never written anything for any actor ever because it's an impractical thing to do. And apart from anything else it gets in between you and what you're trying to create. If you see it in terms of some actor's face or voice, it's hopeless. . . . [Olivier's] reasons for doing it were mixed. One of them, as I've indicated, was that he wanted to keep up with the contemporary bandwagon. Still, it should be remembered it was a daring and courageous thing for him to do then. . . . He was the Establishment actor and he was doing a non-Establishment play by a non-Establishment writer. . . . He did throw it out of balance. The production did suffer in a way, not because of his performance, which was brilliant, but because of the attitude and interpretation of the public, who regarded it as a vehicle for Olivier. The emphasis was too much on him and the other people in the cast, particularly Brenda de Banzie and George Relph, who were outstandingly good, were somewhat overlooked. . . .

The trouble about filming *The Entertainer* was that it was such a theatrical piece that it was almost impossible to transfer it to another medium. . . .

I think a certain self-dislike exists in [Olivier] alongside that feeling about being a grand and important figure in history. . . . I suspect that Olivier has a feeling sometimes that he is a deeply hollow man. That doesn't mean that he *is* a hollow man, but he knows what it's like to feel hollow. And that's why — or it's one of the reasons — he was so good as Archie Rice. Olivier understands that kind of character and his feelings of inadequacy — of being fifth-rate. All comics are ready to duck even when they appear to be aggressively confident, perhaps even more so then. Olivier knows the ready-to-duck mentality.

'John Osborne', *Olivier*, ed. Logan Gourlay
(Weidenfeld and Nicolson, 1973), p. 146-50

Osborne has had the big and brilliant notion of putting the whole of contemporary England on to one and the same stage. *The Entertainer* is his diagnosis of the sickness that is currently afflicting our slap-happy breed. He chooses, as his national microcosm, a family of run-down vaudevillians.

Kenneth Tynan, *A View of the English Stage* (Davis-Poynter, 1975), p. 201-3 (from *The Observer*, 14 Apr. 1957)

At first sight I took Mr. Osborne's play to be a microcosm of contemporary England, with Billie Rice representing departed Edwardian bliss, Archie standing for useless middle-age, and his daughter Jean for crazy mixed-up youth. I am now prepared to modify my claim: I do not think Mr. Osborne meant to cast so wide a net. His object is to show us a single wrecked family, and to suggest that the clue to its disintegration lies in the breakdown of solid Edwardian values. 'They had dignity': and commercialism has destroyed it, as it destroys poor Billie. Of course, Mr. Osborne's nostalgia is not untempered with rage: he is a dandy with a machine-gun in his hands. His people are not happy failures, they are savage failures, and there is rancour in their despair. But what binds them together is the conviction that the present has little to offer them, and the future even less. We made a big mistake over Mr. Osborne. The true hero of *Look Back in Anger* was not Jimmy Porter, but Jimmy's father-in-law. . . . Immediate visible action is not, on the evidence at present available, Mr. Osborne's strong point. All the important events in *The Entertainer* happen off-stage. . . . Mr. Osborne's firmest emotional allegiance is to the past, but his idiom is strictly of the present. . . . The vital inner hollowness that Sir Laurence [as Archie] projects is so authentic as to be almost sickening. The mechanical wink, the slapdash buck-and-wing, the compulsive gin-swilling, the infectious cynicism.

Kenneth Tynan, 'Dandy with a Machine-Gun',
The Observer, 15 Sept. 1957

What makes this a great play — and I use the word advisedly — is Osborne's capacity to capture the texture of family life and, in particular, that of the messy, boisterous, socially disreputable Rices. . . . What, in the end, is most striking about Osborne's play is the way it both echoes the spirit of its time and yet reaches beyond it. It is an attack on the decline of real human values and the advent of a shoddy new opportunistic materialism: the irony is that it was written at the time of a Tory premier who was himself regarded as an old actor-manager. But the play goes beyond the late fifties and says something about the need to recognize that families made up of misfits, nuisances, and bums lead lives of noisy desperation that strikes an uneasy chord.

Michael Billington, *The Guardian*, 6 June 1986

Like all Osborne's best work, this is a play about personal failure, individual desolation, the frustration of the soul into which we are entitled to read the frustration of a community. One of the reasons why Osborne changed the face of the English theatre is that he made passionate personal drama out of a national malaise.

John Peter, 'Reviving a Domestic Drama',
Sunday Times, 15 June 1986, p. 49

If you recalled *The Entertainer* the way I did, as a play about England seen as a dying vaudeville act, or as a play about Suez and national pride, or even as a play about the impossibility of being Max Miller any more, look again. What we have now at the Shaftesbury is nothing less than the English *Long Day's Journey into Night*, a vast rambling family tragedy about death and failure and despair. . . . This is now a company play in which, while Archie roars out his life in four-letter words, the rest of his family try to come to come to terms with their own declining roles in a fast-declining nation. In that sense *The Entertainer* is a rancid *Cavalcade*

Sheridan Morley, 'Doomsday Chic', *Punch*,
18 June 1986, p. 114

The play, in fact, won't hang together and never did. It was always a loose assembly of episodes and attitudes spitted into a semblance of coherence on the gleaming spear of one great performance. . . . To it, I'd say, rather than to *Look Back in Anger*, can be traced most of the really important shifts and developments in British playwriting in the sixties and seventies. It set the generation of playwrights who succeeded Osborne — Peter Nichols, Joe Orton, Peter Barnes, Charles Wood and the rest — on the track of the popular culture and theatre Britain lost with the music halls, and showed the way to a drama which could image the nation to itself, not just the inhabitants of drawing-rooms to the inhabitants of drawing-rooms.

Ronald Bryden, *Plays and Players*, Feb. 1975, p. 22-3

On the Film:

As in *Look Back in Anger*, we are taken out of the emotional cockpit of the flat into the world of shops and pubs and railway stations. The Morecambe locations are conspicuously well used. . . . The writers . . . have not faced the main difficulty. The claustrophobic tautness is not just a stage technique but the means by which the play clinches its emotional grip. Let it relax, and we are left with a series of isolated impressions. . . . The film has a good deal more narrative; and the result, particularly in the second half, is that slabs of incident — the meeting with the impresario, old Billy Rice's death in the wings on the opening night, his funeral, Jean's decision to break with her fiancée — stand out cumbersomely.

Penelope Houston, *Sight and Sound*, 29, Autumn 1960, p. 194-5

See also:

Herbert Blau, *The Impossible Theater* (New York: Macmillan, 1964), p. 213-20.
Gareth and Barbara Lloyd Evans, eds., *Plays in Review, 1956-1980* (Batsford, 1985), p. 56-9.
Hermann J. Weiand, ed., *Insight IV* (Frankfurt am Main: Hirschgraben Verlag, 1976), p. 93-102.

Epitaph for George Dillon

A play in three acts, written (about 1954) in collaboration with
  Anthony Creighton.
First production: Experimental Th. Club, Oxford, 26 Feb. 1957
  (dir. Don Taylor).
First London production: Royal Court Th., 11 Feb. 1958 (dir.
  William Gaskill; with Robert Stephens as George Dillon, Yvonne
  Mitchell as Ruth, Alison Leggatt as Mrs. Elliot, Toke Townley as
  Mr. Elliot), transferred to Comedy Th. (re-titled *George Dillon*),
  29 May 1958 (Mr. Elliot now played by Malcolm Hayes).
First New York production: John Golden Th., 4 Nov. 1958 (dir.
  William Gaskill; with Robert Stephens as George Dillon, Eileen

Herlie as Ruth, Alison Leggatt as Mrs. Elliot and Frank Finlay as Mr. Elliot).

Published: Faber, 1958; in *New English Dramatists*, 2 (Penguin, 1960).

The second act of Epitaph for George Dillon . . . *contains a long duologue which in terms of human contact and mutual exploration is better than anything in Mr. Osborne's later unaided works. One of the participants is Dillon himself, a* farouche *young actor-dramatist currently sponging on a suburban family. . . . Dillon has walked out on his wife, a prosperous actress whom he venomously accuses, à la Jimmy Porter, of having 'betrayed' him. In his new suburban bolt-hole he meets, as Jimmy never did, his intellectual match. This is Aunt Ruth, the family outsider, whose life has hit the emotional doldrums. She has just ended two affairs, one of them with Communism and the other with a young writer skilled in the neurotic art of extorting love by means of pathos. The job of playing Marchbanks to her Candida is temporarily vacant. George volunteers for the part, and the scene in which they come to grips (or, rather, fail to come to grips) is an object lesson in meaty, muscular, dramatic writing. Ruth, the born giver, slowly recognizes in George a born taker. He savages her cliché-ridden family, whom he regards as part of a universal conspiracy to destroy him. . . . George admits to a terrible doubt. He has all the popular symptoms of genius, but perhaps not the disease itself. The admission, however, cuts no ice with Ruth, and George has to console himself by jumping into bed with her teenage niece. Up to this point, apart from a few glaring crudities in the handling of flashbacks, the play is entirely successful — powerful, honest, and transfixing. . . . In the third act George makes one of his plays a provincial hit by spiking it with sex; simultaneously he recovers from an attack of TB and agrees to marry Ruth's niece, who is pregnant by him. He ends in tears. But are they the tears of a good writer frustrated by the commercial theatre and suburban morality? Or the tears of a bad writer who has at last met himself face to face? We are given no clue.*

Kenneth Tynan, *A View of the English Stage* (Davis-Poynter, 1975), p. 212-14, from *The Observer*, 16 Feb. 1958

[Anthony Creighton] had told me about two middle-aged women employed at the debt-collectors who had both taken a kind of appalling fancy to him and of the crude plot he had worked on around this sickly theme. I supplied the title, *Epitaph for George Dillon*, without much enthusiasm. Collaboration with Anthony was less attractive to contemplate than it had been with Stella but it had the advantage of being undisturbed by sexual emotions, at least on my own part. I left the more tedious playmaking passages (which Stella probably called exposition) which Anthony was eager to do and concentrated on those scenes and aspects which interested me, like the entire Ruth-George scene and Barney Evans himself. It was cobbled together haphazardly in this way in less than three weeks. . . . We worked together like a pair of weekend decorators, sloshing away happily and separately, intent on getting the job done as quickly and cheaply as possible. . . . Critics were to point out that someone called Anthony Creighton had imposed a discipline on me which I had been unable to exercise on myself in the writing of *Look Back in Anger*.

John Osborne, *A Better Class of Person*, p. 257-8

The reason George fascinates us is not because we care fundamentally whether good people without talent are more or less valuable to society than the stinker-geniuses who don't give a damn for their fellow-men: we care about George's situation because it gives us insight into his complex personality, his egomania, his sexual frustrations (he prefers older women whom he can lean on financially and emotionally), his haunting doubts of his own value as a man and an artist. In short, George is in several kinds of dilemma, and we feel he is typical of many thoughtful or creative people trying to adjust themselves to the twentieth-century world of retail art and wholesale artists. . . . Robert Stephens's George is near-perfection as he flings his arms out toward life, or shrinks away from it, his head lowered for the assault or his shoulders crumpled with fear. . . . The most obvious mistake is three badly written flashback monologues which take place on a high platform, floating in space. Another is the nature of the first act, which sets the mood and pace for comedy, although the play turns out to be a tragedy.

Mario Amaya, *Plays and Players*, Apr. 1958, p. 23

In *Epitaph* Osborne and Creighton take the germ of a promising dramatic idea — the planting of a mediocre artist into the weed patch of petit-bourgeois suburbia — and spoil most of it by hideous plotting and amateurish dialogue that are symptomatic of their insecure grasp of their theme. . . . The first act is an obvious but effective satiric evocation of the tension and meanness of the representative Elliot domicile. Mrs. Elliot is an able caricature of the typical matriarch of aspidistra-land. . . . Osborne and Creighton never see virtue, as Orwell did, in the stubborn endurance of the basic unit of the British social structure. . . .

In the electric confrontation between George and Ruth (a rebel Elliot, educated, leftist, nonvirginal, and worldly wise), George is the prototypical modern intellectual hemmed in by self-doubt and despondency. He touches Ruth and us. . . . The sexual tension of the scene is remarkable, every bit as powerful as that in the second act of *Anger*, where intense sexuality is manifested as verbal aggression. . . . Osborne is superb in his dramatization of the psychological configurations of modern sexuality. Sex is a cardinal Osborne subject, primarily as symptom and expression of anxiety.

Harold Ferrar, *John Osborne*
(New York: Columbia U.P., 1973), p. 13-16

The World of Paul Slickey

A 'comedy of manners with music' in two acts.
First London production: Palace Th., 5 May 1959 (dir.
    John Osborne; with Dennis Lotis as Jack Oakham, Marie Lohr as
    Lady Mortlake and Adrienne Corri as Lesley), preceded by
    provincial tour.
Published: Faber, 1959.

Jack Oakham, author of the 'Paul Slickey' column in the Daily
Racket, *is sent to Mortlake Hall, home of his father-in-law, Lord
Mortlake. The peer must live five years if his money, in a trust
for his children, is to escape death duties. The paper suspects
that his family may try to conceal his death, and Oakham is to
be present to investigate. Oakham is unhappy with his wife, and
her sister is his mistress. The play comments on such subjects as
Randolph Churchill, the treatment of class in British war films,
and the false sincerity of rock singers. Osborne attacks authoritarian Tory women who support capital punishment in a song,
'Why don't they bring back the axe?', and the evasive
Conservative who sings, 'If your words mean nothing, then your
fingers won't get burned.'*

[The title refers to actual gossip columnists, Paul Tanfield of the *Daily Mail* and William Hickey of the *Daily Express*. Osborne had suffered from the misrepresentations of columnists; Penelope Gilliatt attacked them in 'The Friendless Ones' in *The Queen* in 1960. See Magnus Turnstile, The Death of Paul Slickey', *New Statesman*, 8 April 1966, p. 499-500.]

Its extraordinary dullness may be accounted for by the manifest failure of Mr. John Osborne to make up his mind what he wants to do. He seems in the beginning to have a down against writers of newspaper gossip. This changes into general resentment of popular newspapers; then of popular taste. Before he has made any notable hits on any of these targets he trains his guns against three pairs of adulterers in one of the stately homes of England. Here, again, he cannot escape dullness. He turns, in desperation as it were, to vulgar mockery of a religious funeral. . . . Finally, he falls back on change of sex as a cure for adultery, and the dullness becomes actively boring. The root of the trouble appears to be that Mr. Osborne could not find a workable scheme for his musical comedy and let himself suppose that he could get on without one by scoring off anyone who chanced to excite his displeasure. But his lack of skill in lyric writing soon puts paid to this wild hope.

> 'Extraordinarily Dull *World of Paul Slickey*',
> *The Times*, 6 May 1959, p. 15

This musical play must rank as one of the monuments of ineptitude in the English theatre. Produced by Mr. Osborne himself in the style of a 1923 production of *No, No, Nanette*, it rambled on for hours, although not, understandably, for many weeks. It employed actors and singers of a desperate archness. What it was all about we shall probably never know, for the printed version is more incomprehen-sible than the stage performance.

> *John Whiting on Theatre* (London: Alan Ross, 1966), p.41

[Osborne denounced the hostile reviewers: 'There is not one daily critic in London intellectually equipped to review a play properly' (*New York Times*, 8 May 1959, p. 23). Negative reviews and excerpts from the play are reprinted in *A Night at the Theatre*, ed. Ronald Harwood (Methuen, 1982), p. 135-51.]

The British ruling class, along with all the institutions it has created for its defence and comfort, is about to receive the theatrical trouncing of its life. When John Osborne's musical, *The World of Paul Slickey*, starts its run on the London stage in early May, it's difficult to believe that anything will ever be quite the same again. The families that have guided Britain's destinies (as Osborne puts it) since the South Sea Bubble and the American War of Independence [a reference to a line cut from the printed text]; the Tory Party, the Church, Fleet Street, the 'safe' theatre and film industry; the social, financial, and sexual codes and loyalties of Top People — what a knock the whole set-up takes! . . . For these people, says Osborne to all that have ears to hear, belong to a class that has gone rotten. Whatever ideals of service they once possessed are now corroded into the selfish avoidance of social responsibility — which in turn, inevitably, has killed ordinary humanity too. . . . [If] you compare it with other musicals. . . . there has never been anything with a tenth of the originality, the punch, the sheer cleverness of this show. Only Brecht's *Threepenny Opera* competes, but not successfully.

> Mervyn Jones, '*Paul Slickey* Puts the Establishment
> under the Knife', *Tribune,* 17 April 1959, p. 5

See also:

Richard Findlater, 'The Case of P. Slickey', *Twentieth Century*,
167, Jan. 1960, p. 29-38.

A Subject of Scandal and Concern

A play for television.
Transmitted: BBC, 6 Nov. 1960 (dir. Tony Richardson; with
Richard Burton as George Holyoake, Rachel Roberts as
Mrs. Holyoake, and George Devine as Mr. Justice Erskine).
First stage production: Nottingham Playhouse, 13 Nov. 1962
(in double-bill with *The Sponge Room*, by Willis Hall).
First New York production: New Th. Workshop, 7 Mar. 1966.
Published: Faber, 1961.

[About George Holyoake, the last person prosecuted for blasphemy in Britain.] It concerns a socialist lecturer who was put on trial in 1842 for saying that he did not believe in God, battled against an impediment of speech and the tangles of English law, and was finally borne down by the weight of public prejudice.

The story has been dramatized straightforwardly and fairly competently.

> *The Times*, 7 Nov. 1960

An exceptionally good play. . . . Holyoakes's militant atheism, as portrayed by Osborne, unflinching in its sacrifice for principle, had to be admitted as essentially religious. The remarkable thing was the way Osborne had managed to project himself on to his character and give so strong an illusion of reviving the ambience of the 1840s while preserving Holyoake's obsessional cussedness. . . . The atmosphere of the witch hunt in and around the stuffy little Gloucestershire court was strongly contemporary. . . . Both writing and production had a deceptively simple, gimmick-free quality.

> Maurice Richardson, 'A Triumph of Principle',
> *The Observer*, 13 Nov. 1960

The heart of the play appeared far less concerned with denial of free speech, atheism, or blasphemy, and much more with the difficulties that confront the non-conformist or free-thinker in any society, difficulties which to a lesser degree confront the man or woman out of step in the quasi-Christian Britain of today. If the law no longer prosecutes today's Holyoakes the Church is quick to attempt suppression of the voice of protest or disbelief (Mrs. Margaret Knight has a remarkable story to tell of this) and Society, freely herded by mass-communications, is all too ready with supporting indignation. On the plane of human relationships, there is a plenitude of Mrs. Holyoakes ready with a range of emotional pressures to restore conformity. . . . By all means disbelieve, says John Osborne, but be aware of Man's apparent helplessness; Man it seems cannot live by reason alone, and his atavistic craving for a deity — preferably with sacramental blood — must be assuaged.

> Robert A. Adams, 'Osborne on TV' (letter),
> *The Spectator*, 2 Dec. 1960

Luther

A play in three acts.
First performance: English Stage Co. at Th. Royal, Nottingham, 26 June 1961 (dir. Tony Richardson; with Albert Finney as

Luther, Bill Owen as Hans, John Moffatt as Cajetan and Peter
Bull as Tetzel), transferred to Théâtre des Nations, Paris, July.
First London production: Royal Court Th., 27 July 1961, trans-
ferred to Edinburgh Festival, then to Phoenix Th., 5 Sept.
1961.
First New York production: St. James' Th., 25 Sept. 1963 (dir Tony
Richardson; with Albert Finney as Luther, Kenneth J. Warren
as Hans, and Peter Bull as Tetzel).
Film: script by Edward Anhalt, dir. Guy Green, with Stacy Keach
as Luther, 1973.
Published: Faber, 1961.

*In twelve scenes. Luther becomes a monk in 1506, saying
farewell to his father. The evils of the Roman Catholic church
seen when Tetzel sells indulgences. Luther preaches, holding his
95 theses. Pope Leo X, in hunting clothes, discusses the problems
lems posed by Luther. Debate at the Diet of Worms is followed
by a Knight talking with Luther about his repudiation of the
peasants' revolt he has prompted. Luther is last glimpsed, with
his wife, tired and middle-aged, in 1530.*

It's difficult to pinpoint just how *Luther* started. It's been brewing over a
long period. I wanted to write a play about religious experience and various other things, and this happened to be the vehicle for it. Historical
plays are usually anathema to me, but this *isn't* a costume drama. I hope
that it won't make any difference if you don't know anything about
Luther himself, and I suspect that most people don't. In fact the historical character is almost incidental. The method is Shakespeare's or almost
anyone else's you can think of.

> Osborne, *A Casebook*, p. 66-7, from *Twentieth Century*, Feb. 1961

A puritanical element has always been there in me. I don't think there's
been any change in that in any way. *Luther* was my most obvious
expression of this — until *Judas* [which he says he will write when 'the
time is ripe'].

> Osborne, quoted by W.J. Weatherby, 'Middle-Age of the Angry Young
> Men', *Sunday Times Magazine*, 1 Mar. 1981, p. 35

Luther is a magnificent pageant, sonorous, richly theatrical, illuminating, couched in Mr. Osborne's (and, to do his subject justice, Luther's) strongest prose. The seemingly effortless fluency of Mr. Osborne's writing has its effect not only in the great set-pieces — Luther's sermons or the indulgence sales-talk of the corrupt monk Tetzel — but in much of the quieter, more intimate dialogue, in particular the scenes between Luther and his father. Finest of all, perhaps, is the shining intellectual duel between Luther and the Pope's Legate (beautifully, deeply played by Mr. John Moffatt), in which Luther, alternately cajoled and threatened, stands firm by his tormented conscience. . . .

We at any rate can be certain that *Luther* in terms of pure theatre (in the widest sense of the phrase) enriches Mr. Osborne's reputation and our stage. And Mr. Albert Finney's performance enriches the play. His technical command is astounding: I have never seen gradual ageing so well portrayed. And with his technique goes a passion, a bursting, writhing, conviction of holy righteousness, that takes this performance at one stride to the forefront of anything visible in London today.

Bernard Levin, 'I Salute the Golden Ageing of Albert Finney',
Daily Express, 6 Sept. 1961

The play offers no analysis of the causes of the Reformation, no explanation of Luther's magnetism, not even the picture of an age. It merely shows one man's rebellion against the world into which he was born, and his search for a personal understanding of life, a personal relationship with God. . . . Its style varies to suit the mood of each scene, sometimes even drifting into expressionism. Nothing that is relevant to Luther's experience is omitted, nothing irrelevant to it is allowed in. . . . The seal on *Luther's* excellence is Osborne's language. No one in the English theatre can write prose like him, dramatic prose designed for the voice and the ear, and he has now proved what an adaptable instrument this prose is.

Bamber Gascoigne, 'First Person Singular',
The Spectator, 4 Aug. 1961

Why . . . should John Osborne have wanted to write a play about the founder of Protestantism? I can think of a number of reasons that might have drawn the two men together across the centuries. Luther in Christendom, like Mr. Osborne in the microcosm of the theatre, was a stubborn iconoclast of lowly birth, resentful of authority and blind to compromise. Rather than retract a syllable of his writings he would defy the Pope; one is reminded of Mr. Osborne's brushes with the Lord Chamberlain. To his surprise and alarm, Luther caused an international tumult with his attacks on indulgences, and was hailed as a popular hero by people of whose causes he thoroughly disapproved: is there not something here that might speak to the author of *Look Back in Anger*, embarrassed to find himself dubbed an apostle of social revolution when in fact, like Luther, he preached nothing but revolutionary individualism? 'In many ways, life began for Luther all over again when the world . . . forced him into the role of rebel reformer and spiritual dictator': thus Erik H. Erikson, the author of *Young Man Luther*, a psychiatric study that could have served as the germinal text for Mr. Osborne's play. Dr. Erikson, like Mr. Osborne, seizes on the fact that Luther was plagued throughout his life by constipation, and habitually expressed himself in anal imagery. Oppressed and frequently beaten by his father, he became 'inhibited and reined in by a tight retentiveness'; the celebrated 'revelation in the tower', wherein he first felt himself flooded and illuminated by the Holy Spirit, took place while he was in the privy — 'a revelation', Dr. Erikson adds, 'is always associated with a repudiation, a cleansing . . .'. Once he had solved the riddle of the sphincter, his way was free to solve the problem of man's relationship with divinity. . . . This aspect of Luther, the neurotic haunter of lavatories, is brilliantly conveyed by Mr. Osborne, and as brilliantly linked with the Luther we all know — the fractious, self-lacerating monk who refused to concede that the Church could wash away his guilt, and thus bequeathed to us the chronic Angst of Protestantism. . . .

In form, the play is sedulously Brechtian, an epic succession of tableaux conceived in the manner of *Galileo*; and the graph of its development is likewise Galilean — a rebel against papist dogma publishes heresies, and is asked by velvet-gloved officialdom to recant. The difference is that Luther rejects the demand; all the same, Mr. Osborne's final scene is an obvious echo of Brecht's. . . . The prose, especially in Luther's sermons, throbs with a rhetorical zeal that has not often been heard in English historical drama since the seventeenth century, mingling gutter candour with cadences that might have come from the pulpit oratory of Donne. And it can readily swerve into comedy.

Kenneth Tynan, *A View of the English Stage*, p. 314-16,
from *The Observer*, 9 July 1961

Christians are very poor hands at recognizing Christianity in a drama. . . . In *Luther* they will be (indeed have been) shocked by seeing the Holy Father dressed in the romantic but unreligious habit of a Renaissance huntsman, by a Luther who preaches about a rat gnawing at his private parts in a privy, by Tetzel's sales talk in the market place, by a Reformer whose tongue is literally filthy with vomit. They will fail to notice the astonishing fact that this play . . . leaves as the last thing in the audience's mind the words of Christ, 'A little while and ye shall not see me, and again a little while and ye shall see me', finishing, actually finishing, with a tender and timid hope of immortality. They will overlook how movingly, in an aside alive with emotion, John Moffatt's Papal Legate defends the unity of the Roman Church; they will miss, or at least they missed in Paris, the equally touching unemphatic phrases in which the Staupitz of George Devine recalls the piety of many monks, as they will fail to admire the indefatigable and unattractive resolution with which Mr. Osborne's Luther, racked with disease and tormented by his imagination, holds blindly and violently on to the path his broken feet have dedicated themselves to tread.

> Harold Hobson, 'Sloane Square Surprise',
> *Sunday Times*, 30 July 1961

A play about the Reformation. At the start it unfolds, against a backcloth of the false beauty and harmony of the Catholic Church, a searing indictment of all the agonies inflicted by the Papacy and its prescriptions. Outside a Soviet show trial or a McCarthy witchhunt, few scenes can be more horrific than that of the miserable monks at a mass confessional, inventing sins they have not committed and abjectly pleading for the penance of cleaning out the latrines. . . . The play centres on the struggle within [Luther]; no worthy combatant outside is needed to make the conflict. And who, after witnessing the uncertainty in the mind and heart of such a believer as Luther, will dare arrogate to himself the right to enforce his own certainties with the thumbscrews and the rack of the Inquisition? . . . That a playwright should step with such assurance from his crowded bed-sitting rooms and sleazy music halls on to the stage of world history; that he should have the insight to see Luther as much as a poet as a prophet; and that he should be able to interweave in the ancient drama his own modern strand of relentless astringency — these are further proofs of greatness, if any were still needed.

> Michael Foot, 'Osborne's Luther', *Tribune*, 4 Aug. 1961, p. 6

[Osborne] has laid out a method of production in the text of the play which is concise and clear. But the play has been *produced*. For example, in the printed version Mr. Osborne starts the play with one man simply and straightaway speaking to another. In the stage performance the play begins with a lengthy celebration of mass, or some such nonsense. Again and again, the text of the play demonstrates what is wanted and always the production ignores the instruction or deliberately clouds it. . . . It is very difficult to judge a play when it has been so criminally mishandled as in this production.

> *John Whiting on Theatre* (London: Alan Ross, 1966), p. 37-44

The third act of Osborne's *Luther* is bad. The question is — why is it bad? How could the same author have written the penetrating study of the unhappy genius, which fills the first two acts, and the dull, undramatic, unrevealing farce which, in the third act, is supposed to represent the Peasant War? When the few symbolic peasants appeared waving banners, and singing 'Ein' feste Burg ist unser Gott', the phrase that came to mind was: 'Imitation Brecht.'. . . . The whole attempt is bogus, and therefore every detail resulting from it is bogus. For example, the fact that Osborne's peasants sing in German. If the words didn't matter, why didn't the peasants just hum? If the words did matter, why weren't they in English? I am forced to the conclusion that Osborne has no revolutionary message which will bear putting into English. . . . Osborne's peasants belong to the stage, and nowhere else. Their graceful flag-waving has no relation to anything that goes on, in any real revolutionary movement.

> Alison MacLeod, Letter in *Encore*, No. 34,
> Nov.–Dec. 1961, p. 44-6

The theology and sociology seem to have been left out of it. The three great sermons make three big efforts, but the effects do not reinforce each other. The defiance of the Diet of Worms ought to be a great climax: it is not. Albert Finney, with his superb actor's equipment, gives a wonderful impression of physical growth: but he has not the words to do the same for spiritual growth. One scene does not complement another. The very well written and boldly imagined scene where the wily Italian General of the Dominicans tries, like a clever hostess, to melt Luther's stubbornness, suddenly sounds a strangely false note when the Cardinal indulges in visionary regrets for a Europe divided by nationalist barriers. Surely equally irrelevant, too — though delightful in itself — is the scene showing waspish Pope Leo delayed from hunting by the arrival of the disturbing news from Germany. And in the first act it takes nearly an hour to bring us to Luther's first spoken doubts. In fact, the play, for all its reliance on Brechtian precept, is not well weighted and does not roll us along in consequence.

> Philip Hope-Wallace, *The Guardian*, 28 July 1961

The play itself is hollow. . . . It is hollow in the sense that Osborne's Martin Luther is not a complex, rousing, captivating, charismatic leader: underneath Albert Finney's stinging performance there is only a neurotic mishandled by his father, tortured by inadequate bowel movements, obsessed by images of defecation with which he torments himself and others. . . . [One] reason for this hollowness is Osborne's insistence on making something negative, doubting, unsure under the arrogance, the key to Luther's revolt. Even if that were all there was to it — and I cannot help feeling that this rebellion without cause, or nearly, is more characteristic of Osborne than of Luther — it does not make for strong drama or a convex, alive hero. The very father-son conflict in *Luther* is not commandingly developed. . . . As for the shallowness, it stems from Osborne's inability to make the people, places, and issues come to life. Since Brecht is the model, where is the portrait of an age (real or imaginary, it matters not) that we get in *Mother Courage*; where is the dramatic pot running over with hot bubbling incidents, minor characters, curious inventions? What could be more schematic and stolidly conceived than Osborne's Knight who is supposed to convey Luther's betrayal of the peasants; what could be more perfunctory and unintegrated than the sudden emergence and disappearance of a Mrs. Luther? But, of course, this is Osborne's weakness: he writes dazzlingly about single characters who fulminate in deprecation and imprecation, who can scorch and blast a whole human landscape with their tirades; but when it comes to interrelating characters, presenting complementary or conflicting views with equal vivacity and conviction, Osborne's powers flag.

John Simon, *Uneasy Stages*
(New York: Random House, 1975), p. 21-2

On the Film:

Osborne's play has been adapted (i.e., cut to ribbons) with disastrous effect. . . . Although Stacey Keach gives a sound performance, his American Luther is hardly made more convincing by being saddled with an Irish father (Patrick Magee), a Welsh opponent (Hugh Griffith), and a very English supporting cast (Alan Badel, Robert Stephens, Judi Dench).

Tom Milne, *The Observer*, 16 May 1976

See also:

Notes on John Osborne's *'Luther'* ('Study-Aids', Methuen
     Educational).
Gordon Rupp, 'Luther and Mr. Osborne', *Cambridge
     Quarterly*, 1, Winter 1965-6, p. 28-42.
Marcus Tschudin, *A Writers' Theatre* (Bern, 1972), p. 183-216.

The Blood of the Bambergs

A short play in two acts.

First London production: with *Under Plain Cover*, under joint
title, *Plays for England*, Royal Court Th., 19 July 1962
(dir. John Dexter; with John Meillon as Russell and Vivan
Pickles as Melanie).
Published: with *Under Plain Cover*, under joint-title *Plays for
England*, Faber, 1963.

*Prompted by the kind of publicity which surrounded the mar-
riage of Princess Margaret and Lord Snowdon. In a cathedral
the night before a royal wedding, a Dimbleby-type reverently
describes the scene. News comes that the groom has been killed
in a car crash, and the succession depends on him. A young
Australian photographer sleeping nearby, resembles the dead
prince, so he is persuaded to stand in — by money,
and because he finds the princess attractive. After an intruding
member of the public has killed herself for love of him, five com-
mentators describe the ceremony.*

The form of any Osborne play is always broken, at some stage, by his
rooted icy anger at all our stale, hypocritical compro-mises. In *The
Blood of the Bambergs* . . . his outrage at the mummery of our royal
establishment transcends all form, and turns what might have been a
clever revue sketch into a savagely self-conscious, muddled attack on
the whole spectrum of England's monarchy worship. Dimbleby, Labour
politicians, honest English workmen, the clergy, television and film pre-
sentations, reporters and newspapers — all are subjected to an attack
which veers from crude satire through parody to fantasy. . . . Most of the
set pieces, especially the Minister of Culture's self-revelation, and the
idolatry and suicide of the woman who hides in the royal laundry chute
in order to get a glimpse of her hero, go on far too long. Equally unsatisfactory are the constant in-jokes and half-veiled references to the Royal
Family (and, for all I know, almost anybody else in court or establishment circles). What comes through this badly made sketch is a hatred for
the corrupt, enervated, debilitated world that Osborne conjures up.

Norm Fruchter, *Encore*, No. 39, Sept.–Oct.1962, p. 49-51

Under Plain Cover

A one act play.

First London production: with *The Blood of the Bambergs*,
　　under joint title, *Plays for England*, Royal Court Th.,
　　19 July 1962 (dir. Jonathan Miller; with Anton Rodgers as
　　Tim and Ann Beach as Jenny).
Published: with *The Blood of the Bambergs*, under joint title, *Plays for
　　England*, Faber, 1963.

*Tim and Jenny are a happily-married couple, with two babies.
Their great pleasure is dressing-up, as housemaid and cruel
employer, Girl Guide and boxer, and nurse and patient. They
talk about different kinds of knickers, and who wears what kind.
A reporter finds they are brother and sister: he tells them and
takes Jenny away. Reporters bid for the story. Stanley, the
reporter, arranges a wedding for Jenny and brings Tim to con-
gratulate her. At the end we hear Jenny and Tim are together
again. The play draws heavily 'on an actual case related in
Harry Proctor's book* Street of Disillusion *for the incest theme
and the role of the reporter'* .

John Russell Taylor, *Anger and After*,
revised ed., 1969, p. 59

A broken-backed affair, using the beginning and end of two quite separate plays. At first we watch a suburban married couple as they indulge
happily, even charmingly, in various sado-masochist and fetishist charades. Then it is announced that they are unwittingly brother and sister. . . .
These last scenes . . . have nothing to do with the start of the play. They
could have concerned any incestuous couple. So, in retrospect, the charades are made to seem quite irrelevant.

The presentation of the couple has been praised for its honest realism. It may be that a happily married couple can indulge in sado-
masochistic charades with the almost child-like innocence of these two,
but I doubt it. The lack of any intensified and guilty excitement between
them seems highly improbable.

Bamber Gascoigne, 'From the Head', *The Spectator*,
27 July 1962

It stuns and it shocks. For the first time it brings Genet into England; Mr.
Osborne's married couple in Leicester has clearly been out on the bal-
cony. Their ordinary little home is a veritable *maison des illusions*. . . .
Osborne neither displays nor possesses the perverse delight which bale-

fully shines over the work of M. Genet. He remains a healthy, whole-
some Englishman, with public-school instincts of decency. This makes
him a better man than M. Genet, but not, in this particular case, and in
this case only, so great a poet. The elaborate antiphony . . . on women's
underwear, Directoire knickers, panties, gusset and thread . . . is in the
play, not because Mr. Osborne has been erotically inspired, but because
it is essential to a moral purpose. That purpose is tremendously fulfilled;
and the final figure of the newspaper reporter before the dark and silent
house, self-loathing and abased, Judas before the clock strikes twelve, is
an accusation as powerful in its way as was years ago Zola's. In *Look
Back in Anger* Mr. Osborne marked out a new path in English drama. In
Under Plain Cover he has done it again.

Harold Hobson, *Sunday Times*, 22 July 1962

The pastime of sado-masochism — whereby one gains pleasure from
dominating or being dominated — is deeply ingrained in English sexual
life. . . . The point is that it exists, that it inspires much of our pornography, and that it makes its first overt appearance on the English stage in
Under Plain Cover. . . . Osborne's courage is doubly flabbergasting: not
only does he state the facts about a sado-masochistic *ménage*, he also
refrains from condemning it. . . . This is not only a thriving affair but a
genuine, working marriage: an anal-sadistic relationship need not pre-
clude love. This is perhaps the most audacious statement ever made on
the English stage.

Kenneth Tynan, *A View of The English Stage*, p. 340-41,
from *The Observer*, 22 July 1962

Tom Jones

Film script, based on the novel by Henry Fielding.
Released: 1963 (dir. Tony Richardson; with Albert Finney as
Tom Jones).
Published: Faber, 1964; New York: Grove Press, 1964;
revised ed., 1965.

[The Faber text is Osborne's script; the Grove Press text is taken directly
from the film. 'The Faber text does not contain ten scenes or parts of
scenes to be found in the finished film, but it does include more than
eighty shots cut from the picture' (Robert Hughes, Grove Press ed.,
p. 189).]

Osborne's script concentrates, first, on the salacious elements in Fielding, and, secondly, on the more obvious social satire. Lost, however, is all of that gracious irony, that magnanimous geniality, that vast expanse of verbiage which, so far from boring the reader, gives him ever the sense of being in the presence of a delightful, prolix, mischievous, humane man — the author.

> John Simon, *Private Screenings* (New York:
> Macmillan, 1967), p. 104-6

Tom Jones and a good deal of his age too have called forth a deep response in John Osborne. He seems to have found a real affinity between himself and Henry Fielding. Perhaps he has discovered there in its most positive form the expression of his own essential Englishness. Anyway, Osborne's script is an intelligent, sensitive job. He has reduced the novel's discursive narrative to a brisk, episodic screenplay which falters only over the machinations of Lady Bellaston (the least satisfactory part of the book, in fact). He invents here and there, and only departs radically from Fielding in the final scenes after Tom's imprisonment.

> Philip French, 'Classic Conversion',
> *The Observer*, 1 July 1963

[Dieter Hafner, *Tom Jones: Fieldings Roman und Osbornes Drehbuch, Untersuchungen zu einem Medienweschel* (SSE 105, Francke) is a very thorough comparison of novel and film script.]

Inadmissible Evidence

A play in two acts.
First London production: Royal Court Th., 9 Sept. 1964 (dir.
  Anthony Page; with Nicol Williamson as Bill Maitland,
  Arthur Lowe as Hudson, and Sheila Allen as Liz), revived at
  Royal Court Th., 13 Jan 1965, transferred to Wyndham's
  Th., 17 Mar. 1965.
Revived: Royal Court Th., 12 Aug. 1978 (dir John Osborne;
  with Nicol Williamson as Bill Maitland, Clive Swift as
  Hudson, Elizabeth Bell as Liz, and Deborah Norton as Shirley).
First New York production: Belasco Th., 30 Nov. 1965 (dir.
  Anthony Page; with Nicol Williamson as Bill Maitland),
  transferred to Shubert Th., 8 Feb. 1966.

Revived: Roundabout Th., 23 Feb. 1981 (dir. Anthony Page;
    with Nicol Williamson as Bill Maitland).
Film: script by John Osborne, 1968 (dir. Anthony Page; with
    Nicol Williamson as Bill Maitland, Peter Sallis as Hudson,
    Jill Bennett as Liz, and Eileen Atkins as Shirley).
Published: Faber, 1965.

Inadmissible Evidence *opens with a nightmare court-scene in
which the middle-aged hero pleads, against the odds of a head-
splitting hangover, to justify his life. [Bill Maitland] confesses
that he has always expected to be 'found out', and for the rest of
the play, during two days in his office in the City, we see why
and how he disintegrates. Professionally he can no longer cope
either with his staff or with his clients in their sad cases of
divorce and sexual misdemeanour. The Law Society is after him
for some skullduggery over false evidence, and he can't reach
the people he wants on the phone. He takes pills endlessly and
forgets things. After each blow he rallies, taunts his staff andclutch-
es at his women. But his sexual history of dishonesty, hackneyed
beginnings and even more hackneyed endings is catching up
with him too. His wife nags. The secretary whom he has only
just initiated into the pleasures of sex on the office floor leaves
him. Finally his mistress, to whom he has reached as salvation
throughout the play, runs out on him and the ending is one of
black despair.*

It should be a tragedy of self-discovery, lightened by the intellect and
wit of a man fighting, albeit hopelessly, to shore up the waste he has
made of his life. . . . Maitland is a writer's two-dimensional mouth-piece.
. . .Because Maitland is two-dimensional so are the characters who take
their being from him. . . . Only at the very end, when Maitland sits
deserted in the dark office, is the play briefly moving. . . . It has been
claimed that Bill Maitland is a hero for our time and *Inadmissible
Evidence* a play about our present discontents. If this is the case it serves
to measure how easily confined and acceptable our discontents have
become since *Look Back in Anger*. We have all become older and more
polished.

Mary Holland, 'Where's all the Anger?',
The Observer, 13 Sept. 1964

Inadmissible Evidence has three sources of strength — a blistering rhetoric of spite and disgust, a fascinating self-lacerating protagonist, and a superlative performance by Nicol Williamson. If a play could make it on eloquence and character alone, then this work would be home; but it contains little else in the way of dramatic values, neither discernible structure, coherent progression, variety of portraiture, nor thematic complication. . . . The play, in short, is a monodrama, a highly subjective form demanding a highly subjective approach. Osborne seems partly to realize this, for he begins the play with a dream sequence, showing his hero on trial for having published a 'wicked, bawdy and scandalous object' (i.e., his life). This prologue, however, is generically out of key with the scenes that follow, and is never used or referred to again; instead, the play turns realistic, though the realism is occasionally broken by equally inapposite devices.

Robert Brustein, *The Third Theatre* (Cape, 1970), p. 146-8

Dramatically, *Inadmissible Evidence* handicaps itself by starting at the centre of Maitland's decline and fall. There is no ground from which to mark his descent, no perspective from which to judge its relation to an opposing possibility. Osborne's stock in trade, his great sweeping monologues, are integrated more fully than ever into a total structure, but he is still largely unable to create scenes of true confrontation, clashes of characters, themes, values. Maitland's debacle is a hermetic action, the dreamlike projection of the self to fill the universe.

Richard Gilman, *Common and Uncommon Masks*
(New York: Random House, 1971), p. 114-15

What begins thrillingly — a first act of bawdy brilliance, with a new honesty and objectivity, maturity and compassion — diminishes into time-marking tedium with rambling monologues (still the author's favourite device) and those ritual attacks on conformity which Mr. Osborne cannot restrain himself from making and then — worse — leaving in an already cluttered text. . . .

Though dealing with people at their most pathetic and vulnerable, the play has a generosity of vision in its great central themes, despair at personal inadequacy, fear of oncoming age, fear of up-and-coming youth, fear of death.

Alan Seymour, *The Observer*, 21 Mar. 1965

What dominates the play, though, is the petition in bankruptcy which Osborne files on Bill's (and England's) behalf. Maitland hasn't long been defending himself in the 'dark dock' before it is clear that in his struggle with his hangover, his memory, the pills he can't find, and the paranoid fancies that assault him he babbles for many of England's silent voices. . . . What, through him, these voices have to utter isn't just another outcry against authority; it is a far deeper protest. Though England seems more and more to be talking to herself in a world that takes little notice, they do not want to change; they would rather have England high and dry than England democratic, egalitarian, and efficient.

John Rosselli, 'England on Trial', *The Guardian*, 7 Jan 1965

Maitland is a kind of Willy Loman in striped English serge. Like Arthur Miller in *Death of a Salesman*, Osborne has gathered all the anxieties of his generation into a single image of cathartic collapse. Maitland feels people and things slipping away from him. . . . The difference is that Willy's terror was superannuation by the society to which he belonged. Maitland's is a national dread: his is the generation in power in Britain, he is his own boss, and his sense of failure is mixed up with Britain's inability to cope with the world. He believes, like the posh papers he reads, in planning, automation, 'social engineering' to deal with 'the challenge of the future'; he has no faith that the plans will succeed, the challenge be met. He is no longer confident that the outside world knows or cares about his existence: he only knows it is too much for him. . . .

Ronald Bryden, *The Unfinished Hero* (Faber, 1969), p. 76-80

On the 1981 New York revival:

It's become easier for me to relate to Bill Maitland. The play is much more human this time. It's less strident and more chilling. Bill Maitland is a little smaller, a man more easily seen from the standpoint of human frailty. He's a man to sympathize with. He doesn't ask for sympathy, but he gets it because the audience recognizes in him the human condition. The audience itself is different this time. People are terribly quiet. You know they are disturbed by the play.

Nicol Williamson, quoted by Carol Lawson, 'This Time, Nicol Williamson Feels Closer to Role', *New York Times*, 20 Mar. 1981, III, p. 5

Judged by slide-rule methods of dramatic criticism, John Osborne's *Inadmissible Evidence* has plenty of flaws: it's static, a bit unwieldy in places and doesn't allow much breathing-space to the subsidiary characters. But so much for the slide-rule. All I can say is that seeing the play again at the Court for the first time in 14 years, I found it an overwhelming experience in which the sense of private pain, paranoia and anguish is deeply moving. The first key difference one notices after 14 years is that it now seems an almost totally non-naturalistic play. . . . Osborne's production is at pains to emphasize the dream-like nature of it all. One actress plays three separate clients in whom the hero, Bill Maitland, sees only an extension of his own breakdown. The lights are gradually lowered as the clients talk, giving an impression of the darkness inside Maitland's skull. And Nicol Williamson's own delivery has become much more Beckettian, full of sharp, angular phrases rather than rolling rhetorical periods.

The play does so many things so well. It gives one of the best documented accounts of paranoia I know. . . . It also demolishes the old idea that tragedy is something that happens only to the elevated: Maitland is 'irredeemably mediocre' yet the intensity of his downfall is nonetheless great. It also conveys memorably the fact that Maitland's disease is a helpless longing for all the things from which his own nature excludes him: love, charity, forgiveness, effortless style. . . .

Williamson's performance is also quite astonishing. From the first moments in the dock he is an amalgam of wheedling ingratiation, hypochondria (worrying about glands like 'broken marbles'), sneering defiance. And throughout, much like Beckett's Krapp, he seems to be possessed by some memory of lost happiness as he confronts desertion, betrayal and loss. Knocking over glasses of water, reaching nervously for non-ringing phones and staring at people as if they are figures in a dream ('Who *are* you?' he asks of a homosexual client he half recognizes) he gives us a marvellous manifestation of physical breakdown.

Michael Billington, 'An Essay in Power and Paranoia',
The Guardian, 13 Aug. 1978

On the Film

In filming it we had a clear choice. We could either do a photographed version of the play keeping it to Maitland's office or we could rethink it completely in film terms and show you something of the character's background. We decided on the latter. With a rhetorical writer like Osborne this meant sacrificing a lot of the text — some of the verbal wit is perhaps lost — but I hope we've still kept the concentration of the original and the heroic aspect of the central figure. One of the things that gives me faith in the film is that people identify so closely with Maitland; in New York, particularly, strangers would come up to Nicol in restaurants and tell him how much of the character they saw in themselves.

Anthony Page (director), quoted in 'Anthony Page's Film of
Inadmissible Evidence', *The Times*, 20 May 1969

All the long diatribes have gone, to be replaced by tetchy little outbursts which may be more realistic but reduce the almost-tragic hero of the play to their own size. We are no longer *inside* a man's mind, but outside looking at his snivelling, self-pitying view of himself; and instead of being moved by the fact that nobody seems to pay attention to his inner feelings and hopes, one wonders why one should be asked to sympathize with such a dreary, unprepossessing and self-centered individual who has no time for anyone else. One is, in fact, wholeheartedly on the side of the people who abandon him — which makes nonsense of the whole exercise.

Tom Milne, *The Observer*, 25 May 1969

Maitland, the two-bit solicitor desperately conducting a poll on his own life, seems curiously diminished. He is no longer a giant of a man upended by his capacity to find only shadow in substance and vice versa. Instead, he seems every bit as feeble as those around him, only less capable than they of putting a satisfactory front on things. Williamson's is a magnificent performance, both explosive and controlled, but seen from this point in time Maitland is hollower than before. When he turns on himself, he is splendidly convincing. When he berates others, like his teenage daughter, the eloquence is somehow like an echo. Osborne's rewriting has not taken account of the differences between the early and the late sixties. It seems a little tired in places. . . . The location work is much better than it was, say, in the screen adaptation of *Look Back in Anger*. The dream sequences haunt because of their very greyness. . . . This is a very funny as well as terrifying portrait of failure and breakdown. . . . Maitland's bitter observations on middle-class professional life, particularly on the sexual syndrome commonly known as 'office-girlitis', are frequently irresistible.

Derek Malcolm, 'Grey Eminence', *The Guardian*, 20 May 1969

See also:

John Russell Brown, *A Short Guide to Modern British Drama* (Heinemann Educational, 1982), p. 77-8.
Walter Kerr, *Thirty Plays Hath November* (New York: Simon and Schuster, 1969), p. 46-9.
Benedict Nightingale, *An Introduction to 50 Modern British Plays* (Pan, 1982), p. 305-9.

A Patriot for Me

A play in three acts.

First production: Royal Court Th., London (as a club, to circumvent the Lord Chamberlain's ban on the play), 30 June 1965 (dir. Anthony Page; with Maximilian Schell as Redl and Jill Bennett as the Countess).

Revived: Palace Th., Watford, 4 Dec. 1973 (dir. Stephen Hollis; with Michael Byrne as Redl and Marianne Faithfull as the Countess); Chichester Festival, 12 May 1983 (dir. Ronald Eyre; with Alan Bates as Redl and Sheila Gish as the Countess), transferred to Haymarket Th., Aug. 1983.

First New York production: Imperial Th., 5 Oct. 1969 (dir. Peter Glenville; with Maximilian Schell as Redl and Salome Jens as the Countess).

Film: the play is one of the sources of *Colonel Redl*, 1985 (dir. Istvan Szabo; screenplay: Peter Dobai).

Published: Faber, 1966; with *A Sense of Detachment*, Faber, 1983; in *Landmarks of British Drama: the Sixties*, ed. Roger Cornish and Violet Ketels, Methuen, 1985.

Takes place in Lemberg, Warsaw, Prague, Dresden and Vienna, 1890-1913, in 23 scenes with over 80 characters, and based on fact. Redl, though of low background, is selected to attend the War College. He takes Countess Delyanoff as his mistress. At the end of the first act, he is in bed with a young man, and says 'Why did I wait— so long' . Act 2 opens with the big scene, an annual ball in Vienna where we gradually discover that the apparent women are all men. Redl is blackmailed into spying for Russia, which may have contributed to World War I. He is promoted to head of Intelligence. Found out, he shoots himself, after which it emerges that he was half-Jewish.

A Patriot for Me is based on fact: the story of Alfred Redl is true, if not fully known in Austria even today. . . . The Austro-Hungarian army was one of the most remarkable institutions of modern times. It is almost completely forgotten because the whole basis of its existence was shattered at the end of the 1914 war. . . . The army in a sense was the Empire, the first genuinely international standing army since Roman times. For the career officers and men, the army was their second home. In their profession they were all one, acknowledging allegiance not to a country but to a man, the Emperor. It was the Emperor Francis II who first used the term 'Ah! But is he a patriot for me?'. . . . The Army was a body of Imperial patriots. It was also democratic. The real commanding was done by those who had risen to the top more often than not by merit. . . . This, then, was the institution in which Lt. Redl, a young Galician lacking wealth, influence, or connections, began his career.

Programme note

I had for years been wanting to write a play about homosexuality and the whole ambiguity of it. I began with the image of something on the stage — which is how I usually start a play. About eight years ago I was talking to George Devine, the director of the Royal Court Theatre, and Christopher Isherwood. I told them I wanted to do this play in which there would be an absolutely ambiguous scene — terribly baroque, with everybody on the stage looking marvellous. And for as long as possible the audience mustn't know what is really going on — that, in fact, they are seeing a drag ball. Devine thought it a marvellous idea, and that was that. Then about four years later I was reading books about the Austro-Hungarian Empire, and I kept stubbing my toe against this little footnote about Redl. It seemed fascinating and I followed it up. I found a bad biography by someone, and then I got all sorts of things from the British Museum. But there isn't very much on Redl; it's mostly speculation. Which is odd because it was a *cause celèbre* at the time, and in Central Europe it is still one of the most famous of all scandals. . . . The two things — the homosexuality and the period — came together. Suddenly it made sense. . . . It *is* more detached. That's because it had been around in my mind for so long. It was also the first time I'd ever tackled anything which had the elements of a thriller. I had a clear narrative and certain facts to put over, which I don't usually have to bother with. That makes for a certain distance, perhaps. . . . [Homosexuality] still interests me. In my profession as an actor, I've been surrounded by queers; betrayed by them and disliked by them, and have had friends who were queer. It's not a particular obsession, it's just something one lives with.

Osborne, quoted by A. Alvarez, 'John Osborne and
the Boys at the Ball', New York Times,
28 Sept. 1969, II, p. 1, 5

Osborne's picture of the Empire is both historically based and imaginary. The aspect which he has selected, the anti-Semitism, the complex racial and social snobberies, the blindness and the ruthlessness, are all chosen with a purpose. It is a believable empire, but it is very definitely Osborne's empire. Compare it with the world conjured up in Musil's

novel *The Man without Qualities* and you will see how strikingly different the same historical world can appear to different writers. Compare it
on the other hand with Musil's *Young Torless* and you can see that there
is a connection. Indeed, Musil's cadet school is much nastier and more
violent than anything Osborne depicts.

James Fenton, 'A Patriot's Last Refuge', *Sunday Times*, 15 May 1983

[Osborne] misses many opportunities for satire because the tone is
wrong. These are Prussian, not Austrian, soldiers. In Vienna, callousness
and brutality were covered by a veneer of geniality and false charm. . . .
To appreciate Osborne's failure to re-create convincingly this alien environment one must read (or, better, see) Molnar's *Olympia:* a scathing
satire exposing social hypocrisy and military stupidity, conveyed deliberately and misleadingly in the guise of a glittering, glamorous boule-
vard comedy. . . .

His love-hate relationship with Alfred Redl — expressed eloquently
by Redl himself — finally prevents the play from transcending melodrama and soaring to the heights of tragedy.

Frank Marcus, 'After the Censor', *Sunday Telegraph*,
9 Dec. 1973, p. 16

A Patriot for Me is about as unnecessary a play as I have ever seen. If
you want to find out about the curious story of Colonel Alfred Redl . . .
you can read *The Panther's Feast* by Robert Asprey and find out much
more that way. If you want an imaginative re-creation of the splendour
and misery of life in the Imperial Austrian army, a novella like
Schnitzler's *Lieutenant Gustle* will prove incomparably more revealing.
If you want to learn about homosexuals, there are by now hundreds of
works of fiction, drama and even poetry that will afford you keener
insights. . . .

A Patriot for Me seems to deal with ambition and self-indulgence
fighting it out against the background of similarly schizoid but also nar-
row-minded and corrupt society. It is some kind of dance on top of the
volcano, some sort of *Walpurgisnacht* hurtling into *Gotterdammerung*,
in which social orders, races, sexes, even fellow homosexuals oppose,
torment and persecute one another — but of all these things Osborne
tells you no more than a high-school sex orientation lecture tells about
human relations. . . .

You might expect a play whose high point is a drag ball to be a bore;
what you would not expect is that even the drag ball is a drag.

John Simon, *Uneasy Stages*
(New York: Random House, 1975), p. 218-20

45

One would have thought that the Redl affair was theatrically fool-proof, if only at the level of middlebrow melodrama, but it can't as it turns out survive the almost complete absence of genuine period flavour, or an exposition which crawls forward interminably like a centipede. Possibly the play enshrines political or psychological insights which justify a technique not to be judged by humdrum naturalistic standards, but if so I failed to discover them; and judged by those standards it is a botched piece of work. . . . Haziness is to be found at the very heart of the play. What is it all supposed to prove? Cut is the branch that might have grown full straight, presumably; but as presented here, Redl is a conventional and rather dull careerist who apart from his homosexuality is perfectly willing to love by the standards of the society which ultimately condemns him. Without a more significant clash of values, his downfall is the theme, not for a tragedy, but only for a racy anecdote — unless, that is, we are meant to find more to admire than to deplore in the outlook of the Austro-Hungarian military caste. There is room for fruitful ambivalence here, I suppose; but what actually comes across is indecision, as though the author were unwilling to think too hard about the nature of his material.

John Gross, 'Rebels and Renegades', *Encounter*, Oct. 1965, p. 42

Osborne has treated the story in a more-or-less documentary style in twenty-three short scenes. This is really a very lazy and rather ineffectual way of writing a play, especially when as here, some of the scenes are only of marginal relevance. It is even worse when there has to be a scene change at the end of almost ever scene, and we are either kept waiting before a dropped curtain or entertained, rather against our will, by the pleasant music of Tibor Kunstler's *zigeuner* violin.

B.A. Young, *The Mirror up to Nature* (Kimber, 1982), p. 34-6

It throws up a muddled welter of serious issues, depravity and corruption being well to the fore among them, but very little in the way of coherent intention is discernible in its own peculiar mix of moral fervour and poorly-cloaked prejudice. . . . Every imaginable form of paranoia imbues the confusions of Osborne's pageant; we would like to believe it belonged to Redl and his society, but the inescapable signs are that it is also the playwright's. . . . No great percipience is needed to grasp that something is being said about the state of the nation, our nation, immediately post-Philby England.

Alan Jenkins, 'Fear and Loathing in Vienna',
Times Literary Supplement, 19 Aug. 1983

Chandeliers, rococo, champagne: a ring of couples, elaborately gowned and uniformed, sway fondly as a pair of rollicking singers prance through Mozart's duet for Susanna and Figaro. It is a Viennese ballroom at the turn of the century and, as another medalled and monocled figure arrives, his hostess sweeps down to welcome him, superb in white satin, throat and bosom blazing jewels, ostrich fan wafting majestically. Some pretty rouged and feathered creatures flock inquisitively after her, hanging giggling on arms oddly sinewy in their long white gloves. She pats their bony rumps and shoulders indulgently, exchanges courtesies with the newcomer, then casually lights up a cigar, rolling it expertly in military hatchet-jaws. Looking about to make introductions, she beckons forward a shyly hovering figure in Turkish harem costume. Lowering her yashmak, the houri reveals a bristling moustache. 'Colonel Redl,' says the queen of the revels in George Devine's silkiest rasp, 'I believe you know Major Steinbauer?'. . . Without its climactic evocation of high Hapsburg queerdom at its annual drag ball, *A Patriot for Me* would be, more or less, a sentimental, high-flown piece of propaganda for the rights of a noble and oppressed minority. Osborne's ball scene is not only magnificently theatrical, the best thing in his play, but its centre, its validation, the image from which all else takes perspective and completeness. It is funny, compassionate, grotesque, humane and defiant. . . . Osborne has taken queerness as his subject precisely as Nabokov took the love of pubescent girls or Henry James the *donée* of American innocence in Europe. He has rendered it for all it is worth, for its exoticism, spectacle, irony and sentiment: for its *interest*.

Ronald Bryden, *The Unfinished Hero* (Faber, 1969), p. 81-5

Today its journalism of life in the homosexual underworld of pre-1914 Vienna seems less interesting than the character of the blackmailed spymaster Alfred Redl who let an empire fall rather than betray his own nature. A true Osborne hero, he protects himself with passion, cunning and bitchery against a world which he sees as a conspiracy to do him down unless he does it down first.

Ronald Bryden (on a production in Bath), *The Observer*, 25 Oct. 1970

Osborne's intention was to show the pressures exerted on sexual deviants by social prejudice; that he was not blaming the queer but the society that outlaws queerness. . . . If [Redl] has to choose between his identity as a homosexual and his identity as a patriot, he prefers the former, as the title boldly declares; moreover, he does so without the faintest glimmer of hesitation or regret. It is here we reach the play's essential originality and audacity. Not only does it repudiate loyalty to Freud and loyalty to country (the twin bastions of Western civilization), its hero neither pities himself nor invites our pity. . . . Redl is an unsentimentalized queer, ambitious, sex-loving and quite unapologetic. For the first time in Western drama, we are asked to identify with a queer not because he is charming or tragic or a genius but simply because he is queer. And the gaudy, notorious set-piece of the Viennese drag ball is there to make things harder for us — to challenge our liberalism by confronting it with queerdom unabashed and impenitent, to remind us that the camp world at which we tolerantly laugh is also the world that our penal code imprisons.

> Kenneth Tynan, 'Missing Osborne's Point', letter in
> *The Observer*, 18 July 1965

In its voluptuous theatricality and constant relation of the individual to society, it is one of Osborne's richest works. Originally it was assumed to be a play about homosexuality. . . . The question which passionately concerns Osborne is precisely what the individual owes to the state and what he owes to himself. In the first act, Redl is a rigid, poker-backed puritan suppressing his natural instincts because he believes he is living in a complex society and owes it his undivided attention: subsequently he surrenders to his queerness and unhesitatingly sacrifices his country's needs to his personal happiness. He become a patriot for me; and his priorities, Osborne suggests, are absolutely right. . . . [Osborne] has always been a poet rather than a committed political figure and the virtues he has constantly endorsed are those of friendship, private loyalty, and emotional candour. From that point of view *A Patriot for Me* is a logical extension of all his previous work. But it also has that perennial ambiguity that seems to enrage Osborne's critics: just as, in *A Sense of Detachment*, he satirized women's lib. (as an institution) while offering the most moving speech I've ever heard about the pain and agony of being a woman, so here he launches a blistering attack on certain aspects of homosexuality while suggesting no man-woman relationship ever captures its physical intimacy. And it is typical of his subversive irony that Redl, the man who puts happiness first, ends up with a bullet in his brain.

> Michael Billington, *The Guardian*, 5 Dec. 1973, p. 12

Garland [Artistic Director of Chichester Festival] calls the piece a play about 'the collapse of empire', examining at several removes 'the English Puritan consciousness', with Osborne envisioning a society 'so pleased with itself and so overdressed that it cannot see what is happening before its very eyes'. Ronald Eyre, the play's director, sees the play in simpler, more elemental terms. For him, *A Patriot* is about concealment: Redl conceals his religious origins and his sexual make-up to advance high in intelligence: blackmailed, he succumbs and finally takes the gentleman's way out. 'Lying is about as old as God. And that's what *A Patriot* deals with'. . . . Garland recalls his memory of the drag ball scene: 'I thought it very unsettling. One elite masquerading as another: it was the one day of the year which they experienced without shame and with a feeling of defiance. I was prepared to be sympathetic and then I discovered these people did not need my sympathy'.

Nicholas de Jongh, 'A Dubious Patriot for Chichester',
The Guardian, 10 May 1983, p. 9

See also:

Valerie Aymand, 'Duty and Patriotism Clad in Shining White', *Théâtre et Politique*, ed., Jean-Paul Debax and Yves Peyré (Toulouse University, 1984), p. 139-47.

Alan Seymour, 'A Maturing Vision', *London Magazine*, Oct. 1965, p. 75-9.

Alan Sked, 'A Patriot for Whom?: Colonel Redl and a Question of Identity', *History Today*, 36, July 1986, p. 9-14 [factual background].

A Bond Honoured

Play in one act.

First production: National Th. at Old Vic, 6 June 1966 (dir. John Dexter; with Robert Stephens as Leonido and Maggie Smith as Marcela) in double-bill with Peter Shaffer's *Black Comedy*.
Published: Faber, 1966.

In a tank of blind walls, a cry of cloaked players sit ranged in shadow, the women fanning like carp. Two actors come forward: a servant and his master, a curly, half-naked voluptuary from a Caravaggio orgy. Restlessly circling, curling ripe, angry lips, the master lashes with his tongue at the servitor and, flinging back his head, at invisible watchers at windows and balconies above. Look, he shouts at them, listen closely, attend to me. Spurning the earth like a scorpion, he carves on the darkness a Blake figure of metaphysical defiance, fist raised at something in the sky beyond them. An unseen ballad singer has already told in lamenting Arab harmonics, at what. This is Leonido, who strikes back at the sun. Out of the conventions of sixteenth-century Spanish drama, in other words, John Osborne has hewed in A Bond Honoured *the perfect Osborne hero. Using the bare open courtyard of the Madrid* corrales, *the anonymous space which could represent at once Europe, the world, heaven and hell, he sets before us the pure human rebel: a protagonist who, liberated from plot and proscenium, carves himself out of eternity. On this stage, freed from the determinism of settings, relationships, alteration by events, he can pursue untrammelled, statically himself, the essential Osborne dialogue: with his nature, the audience, with God and history. . . . [Leonido's] final crucifixion becomes an act of humanist defiance. Having explored his nature beyond the Christian bounds, Leonido takes responsibility for his own debts. No one else will be crucified for* his *sins. . .*

A Bond Honoured *in performance is marvellously theatrical. Around a superb baldaquin of thorny iron by Michael Annals, John Dexter has directed his cast into the plasticity of flamenco dancers, using semi-abstract mime for the moments of violence — blows which fell without connecting, red scarves for head-wounds. Above all, there's Robert Stephens carrying further as Leonido the sculptural technique he mastered for* The Royal Hunt of the Sun: *part-dancer, part-athlete, fixing each posture in bronze.*

Ronald Bryden,'John Osborne's Perfect Hero', *The Observer*, 12 June 1966

In 1963, Kenneth Tynan, Literary Manager of the National Theatre, asked me if I would adapt *La Fianza Satisfecha* by Lope de Vega. It was in three acts, had an absurd plot, some ridiculous characters and some very heavy humour.What did interest me was the Christian framework of the play and the potentially fascinating dialectic with the principal character. So I concentrated on his development (in the original he rapes his sister in the opening moments of the play without any preparatory explanation of his character or circumstances) and discarded most of the rest, reducing the play to one long act. *A Bond Honoured* is the result.

Osborne, 'Note', *A Bond Honoured* (Faber, 1966), p. 9

It is a work of genius which will live as long as the English language.

Osborne has used Lope de Vega's forgotten play as Shakespeare used the original *Hamlet,* giving the story a significance that is his alone. We can forget about the de Vega play, which practically nobody knows; but there is a reason why Osborne worked from it. The peculiarly Spanish atmosphere and outlook — intense, ferocious, uncompromising — colour the whole conception. . . . Irresponsible in the eyes of others, [Leonido] is responsible to himself. He reserves the right to judge, and inflicts on himself the harshest judgment. He honours his bond. On the de Vega text, as on a palimpsest, Osborne has written message after message. Leonido is Mozart's Don Giovanni, he is Dostoyevsky's Stavrogin, he is Camus' Outsider, and he is unmistakably the Osborne Man — Jimmy Porter and Bill Maitland in the perspective of eternity. . . .

Osborne's language, always vivid and exciting and never more so than in this play, has gradually acquired two other qualities not impressively manifest: it is intellectually tough and solid, and it is poetic in imagery. Here is the ring of greatness.

Mervyn Jones, 'Osborne and the Critics', *Tribune,* 17 June 1966, p. 15

Osborne seems to have gone to work more in a spirit of self-indulgence than of re-interpretation. . . . What we get [is] the Osborne ego raised to a pitch of delirious omnipotence. . . . The spectacle of gratuitous insult, sexual humiliation and physical cruelty needs a good deal more wary handling and intellectual justification than it did a few years ago.

'Revival Arrives Too Late after 350 Years', *The Times,* 7 June 1966, p. 14

Intellectually this adaptation is an unholy mess, unholy in the truest sense of the word. And artistically it is, accordingly, an abortion, a monstrous aberration. . . . An adaptation which reaches such degrees of confusion makes the actors' tasks well-nigh impossible.

Martin Esslin, 'Obscurity Envelops All', *Plays and Players,* Aug. 1966, p. 22

[The negative overnight reviews prompted an outburst from Osborne.] The gentleman's agreement to ignore puny theatre critics as bourgeois conventions that keep you pinned in your soft seats is a thing that I fall in with no longer. After ten years it is now war. Not a campaign of considerate complaints in private letters but open and frontal war that will be as public as I and other men of earned reputation have the considerable power to make it.

Osborne, telegram to *The Times,* 9 June 1966, p. 14

51

See also:

Geoffrey Morgan, ed., *Contemporary Theatre* (London Magazine
    Editions, 1968), p. 21-6 [collects five reviews].
Daniel Rogers, ' "Not for Insolence, but Seriously": John Osborne's
    Adaptation of *La Fianza Satisfecha'*, *Durham University Journal*,
    1968, p. 146-70 [a definitive comparison of the two texts, concluding
    that 'the meaning is radically altered and becomes extremely
    mysterious'].

Time Present

Play in two acts
First production: Royal Court Th., London, 23 May 1968; transferred
    to Duke of York's Th., 11 July 1968 (dir. Anthony Page; with
    Jill Bennett as Pamela).
Published: with *The Hotel in Amsterdam*, Faber, 1968.

*Pamela, an actress in her thirties, is staying with an efficient
woman Labour M.P., Constance. Pamela is confused, though
reluctant to admit it, drinking heavily, upset by her visits to her
dying father, Sir Gideon Orme, once famous as an actor. At the
end of Act 1 news comes of his death, and Act 2 takes place on
the day of a memorial service for him some weeks later. There
are six minor characters: Edith, Pamela's mother, divorced for
20 years but now sharing the sick-visiting; Pauline, her daughter of 18 by a second marriage; Edward, a handsome, arrogant
womanizer and admirer of Pamela; Murray, Constance's lover;
Abigail, Pamela's sister, a more successful actress than she; and
Bernard, Pamela's agent, who takes her off for a holiday at the
end.*

In a London flat, white, modern and smart as an ice cube, two expen-
sively dressed women converse in clichés colourless as the decor. 'She's
always in the papers.' 'It's not exactly my subject.' 'You're her friend —
52

she needs friends.' Their talk covers a world of success in politics and the theatre. . . .

[Pamela] enters, and starts heaping scorn on contemporary Britain — on the pot-smoking young, unwashed actors and 'happenings', socialism ('Striding into the Seventies with Labour — you must be joking') and high taxes. . . . In *Time Present* Osborne comes as near as possible for him to writing a run-of-the-mill play, but shows a new theatrical craft and objectivity. . . .

Arrogant, vulnerable, caustic, [Pamela] lays about her with the gusto of a feminine Jimmy Porter. 'You're all in show-business now', she tells Constance, 'all beating the drum. Orme was never in show-business.' She's wonderfully bitchy about a tall, Castrophile rival actress whose eyes are always being admired for their Garboesque mystery — 'It's nothing but myopia' — and her actor boyfriend who's had his nose altered for his one film-epic. The weakness, as usual with Osborne, is that none of these subordinate characters begins to match Pamela in reality. Except for Katharine Blake's intelligent, touching Constance, they're too perfunctorily introduced to create any real conflict or plot — the play drifts from one inconsequent diatribe by Pamela to another, sustained only by the vigour and venom of their writing. Still, for once Osborne's created a full-length, rounded character which, while able to work off a good deal of his own wit and spleen, can't be mistaken for an avatar of himself. Pamela is, herself, sufficiently spiky and pathetically individual to make an impersonal point about the necessity and loneliness of egotism in a society whose only shared values are fashionable trivia. You aren't commanded to like her, only to respect and pity her. Unlike Jimmy Porter, she refuses to pity herself — in this if nothing else, *Time Present* is Osborne's most mature, least self-indulgent play.

Ronald Bryden, 'Daughter in Revolt',
The Observer, 26 May 1968, p. 30

When at length the arrival of various other people breaks up [Pamela's] self-indulgent examination of motive, the bout of destructive honesty on the poor creature's part striking sparks off the well-armoured committee woman makes pretty absorbing theatre. By the time the bad news comes from the hospital that the father is dead we feel we know almost as much about this character as about Ibsen's Hedda. But then nothing much happens. There is an unwelcome pregnancy, a fastidious refusal to pinch another woman's lover, some fairly funny in-jokes at the expense of theatre people and a piano exit. It is clear that the M.P. will get on better without her, but she is at best a foil. As from so many of Mr. Osborne's plays one comes away with the memory only of a monologue.

Philip Hope-Wallace, *The Guardian*, 24 May 1968

One might say — and some have — that this is a character-study, not a play of action at all. But characters are studied dramatically by their inter-action with other characters, and there are no other characters in *Time Present*, just names and jobs to sit about and be talked at. Nor does the character who is being studied in any way change. She sustains the loss of a father (offstage), becomes pregnant (during the interval), and continues to talk on and on, mostly about what she dislikes, and to drink champagne. One might say, 'At last John Osborne has written a part for an actress', as if he had never written Phoebe Rice, and as if that alone were sufficient to make a play. In any case, Pamela, his heroine, isn't a very good part for an actress. . . .

I myself think that the theme of the play is the one Osborne has already stated in his Introduction to *The Entertainer*, the death of 'a significant part of England'. The offstage father, an actor just older than the century, represents a style, a standard, a way of living, a way of acting, from which our present time has degenerated. Nothing else is as real — every character and event is judged by him — and when he is dead, only unreality is left.

John Bowen, 'Remembrance of Things Past',
London Magazine, Aug. 1968, p. 89

A long, dyspeptic bellyache about contemporary society that might easily have been put together by Hugh and Margaret Williams with the advice of that pair of ideological bookends, Peter Simple and Malcolm Muggeridge. . . .

Such positive values as [Pamela] possesses are a respect for style and a hatred of vulgarity, neither of which she exemplifies in any major degree. . . . Judging from what she quotes out of his scrapbook, though, Sir Gideon sounds like a pretty inadequate shrine for her to worship at. Like Jimmy Porter's devotion to Mrs. Tanner and the memory of his father, and Archie Rice's grief over the departed Billy, Pamela's attachment to her father, while affecting, is a cover-up for her own inadequacy, an excuse for inaction, and the source of a constant, and debilitating, sentimental undertow. One is tempted to view the play as a personal allegory explaining Osborne's own inextricable involvement with a society — or rather a small segment of a society — that he hates, but which rewards him for expressing this hatred. Seen in this light, it suggests that he would rather stand there insulting the fascinated minotaur than find a clue that would take him out of the labyrinth. For one feels that this is not so much the winter as the après-ski of the author's discontent.

Philip French, *New Statesman*,
31 May 1968, p. 737-8

It is eery, how history closes the circle: twelve years to the month after Osborne's *Look Back in Anger* opened the new era of British drama, the curtain rises at the self-same spot to reveal his latest play *Time Present*; and what does the curtain reveal? The exact replica of that elegant drawing room set, those elegant uppercrust characters, that creaking exposition, that corny, melodramatic plot that were the birthright and the bane of the kind of dreary play which *Look Back in Anger* was supposed to have finished off once and for all time. And what is more: the angry young man whose wit struck terror into the ranks of the philistines now releases a flood of jokes directed against teenagers, the *avant garde*, hippies, happenings, action painters, artistic experimenters, and appeals to those sections of his audience who nod approvingly when the characters with whom they identify on the stage hold forth about high taxation and Parliament spending their well-earned money, who bellow with laughter when someone mentions some progressive fool who goes around with coloured gentlemen who are 'very *New Statesman*', and refers to Italians as 'wogs'. Thus do the angry young men of 1956 turn into the Edwardian high Tories of 1968, the iconoclasts of yesteryear into the satisfied upholders of established values of today. *Time Present* is an interesting play, interesting as a symptom of our return into what might become an era of neo-Victorian values. . . .

There is a hint of the true power of Osborne also in the central theme of the play: the latent, suppressed, subconscious Lesbian relationship between the two women which they do not want, or do not know how to face, and which drives them to alleviating spasms of hostility and attraction. But, alas, this really fascinating subject for a play is barely developed.

Martin Esslin, 'Anger, Twelve Years on', *Plays and Players*, July 1968, p. 24-5

The Hotel in Amsterdam

Play in two acts.

First production: Royal Court Th., London, 3 July 1968 (dir. Anthony Page; with Paul Scofield as Laurie, Judy Parfitt as Annie, Isabel Dean as Margaret, Joss Ackland as Gus, David Burke as Dan, and Susan Engel as Amy), transferred to New Th. on 6 Sept. and to Duke of York's Th. on 12 Dec.

Television transmission: ATV 'Sunday Night Theatre', 14 Mar. 1971 (with Paul Scofield as Laurie, Jill Bennett as Annie, and Isabel Dean as Margaret).

The Hotel in Amsterdam

Published: with *Time Present*, Faber, 1968.

Three couples in a first-class Amsterdam hotel: 'they are all fair-ly attractively dressed and near or around forty but none mid-dle-aged. In fact, they are pretty flash and vigorous looking' (87). Audiences at first are intended to be uncertain about who's who, their jobs, who is with whom, whether or not they are mar-ried. They have run from KL, a tyrannical film producer, and childishly relish their escape: belonging to KL is what holds them together. Laurie is a writer who says 'I am quite certainly the most boring man you have ever met in your lives' (127). He describes Annie as 'the most dashing, romantic, friendly, play-ful, loving, impetuous, larky, fearful, detached, constant woman I have ever met' (139). Annie's husband is Gus, a film-editor. He is the butt of the group, a hypochondriac and possible homosexu-al. Dan is a painter, an 'orangutang' (110) to Margaret, the 'earnest chimpanzee' (110). Amy, KL's secretary, is 'an unneu-rotic fallow deer' (109). All is calm and subdued, with little action, character being revealed through talk, not behaviour. In the last quarter Gillian, Laurie's unhappy sister-in-law, sudden-ly arrives, Laurie and Annie discover their love for each other, and news comes that KL has killed himself.

Hotel in Amsterdam is based on germs of things that happened, but also on things that never happened, and when I watch rehearsals I'm aston-ished how unfamiliar it is to me. I mean I get the chill of it, but I think the old process of conversion has gone to work. . . . Nowadays almost everyone is tainted with show business. Dockers are interviewed in the streets, and writing a play about show-biz people isn't the kind of 'in' experience that it used to be. At one time theatrical folk only spoke to other theatrical folk, but today social contacts are much freer. We're all in show-biz now. It isn't a closed metaphor any more.

'John Osborne Talks to Kenneth Tynan', *The Observer*, 30 June 1968, p. 21

It is a sort of tone-poem, reflecting mood and atmosphere — the mood of a group of six friends abroad, all self-conscious and a bit jaded, film people unsuccessfully trying to forget the pressures from which they are escaping. . . . It is, characteristically, still lacking in dramatic economy. It could all have been done in less than half the time. . . .

[Laurie] *is* a character, with his prejudices, his mistrust of the world outside his circle of friends, his fear of spiritual impotence, his anxieties about becoming older and staler, his laziness and his unexpected moments of generosity, his self-pity, affection and bitter humour. . . . The other characters hardly come to life at all. The three women of the party have very little to say for themselves. . . . [Dan] is only a good listener; and that leaves Gus, fussy, rather proper, inclined to organize others while still being anxious to please them. It is an oddly static characterization: every line Gus speaks seems to be making the identical set of points about him. He doesn't have the capacity to surprise, to do the unexpected (yet consistent) thing that would render him more fully human. Perhaps it's because he, like the other characters, exists only in relation to, indeed in the eyes of, Laurie.

Benedict Nightingale, 'Creative Process?', *Plays and Players,*
Sept. 1968, p. 14-15

Osborne and Scofield's flashes break through a hypnotic miasma of boredom, a tale of bores being bored. . . . Hiding from their boss in a dull Dutch hotel, they can think of nothing to do but eat, drink and sneer at 'bank managers dancing together'. . . . Though overly concerned with matters of vulgarity and stylishness, Osborne seems unable to express these indefinables dramatically.

D.A. N. Jones, *The Listener,* 11 July 1968, p. 59-60

Except for Laurie's sad declaration of love for his best friend's wife — which constitutes one of the most affecting scenes in recent theatre — there are no moments of truth, no epiphanies, no sense of anything dawning on these people, only lassitude come home. . . . I do feel that [Osborne's] at a stage — cyclical in his career — where he's working too close to his material. Put together, tightened up, drained of dramatic contrivance, *Time Present* and *The Hotel in Amsterdam* would not only complement each other, bringing out their individual strengths and eliminating their separate weaknesses, but would make a powerful joint statement on our times and one hell of an evening in the theatre.

Philip French, 'The View Lengthwise', *New Statesman,*
12 July 1968, p. 59-60

The best contemporary play in London: the richest in wit, the most arresting in mood, the most accomplished in performance, and (what is still more important) the most far-reaching and haunting in resonance. . . . It is about fear, the fear, sometimes well-founded but more often not, that seizes people in middle life, when the future no longer seems bright

and certain before them. It is about friendship. It is about goodness. . . .
The play also, it seems to me, is about England. For England, too, is
now in show business. The country may be going to the devil, without
confidence and without ideals, but it has the best entertainment, the best
actors, the best theatre in the world. We are always saying so. I do not
think that this satisfies Mr. Osborne, for he is devoted to England with a
passion that is almost frightening. He is not one of those patriots who are
vocal in praise of our blood and state — but who live in Switzerland. He
is tortured by our decline, and angry at our lazy and selfish complacen-
cy; they wring from him the cries of a true distress.

Harold Hobson, 'Prisoners of Freedom',
Sunday Times, 7 July 1968, p. 49

Sameness and monotony were oddly symbolized for me in England this
summer as soon as I saw the curtain going up on *The Hotel in
Amsterdam*. For an instant I wondered if I was back at another Osborne
play, *Time Present*, which I had seen only a few days before. The settings for both plays — a chic London flat and a chic hotel suite — were
almost identical. Both of them in their antiseptic whiteness suggested a
hospital operating room, the tubular steel furniture as sleek and shiny as
surgeons' instruments. And both — deliberately done this way by the
same team of designers — were handsome but dehumanized back-
grounds for dissecting the human psyche. Osborne, I said to myself, is in
trouble: he needs a change of scenery. The same glib, gifted people in
the same upper echelons of the entertainment world inhabit both of his
new London plays. . . . In his latest plays he neither sparkles, breaks our
hearts, nor stings us with his irate invective. Osborne possesses a valuable voice of protest which is stuck now on a tired note of futility in the
hothouse world of entertainment.

Tom Prideaux, 'Johnny's Dying One-Note', Life, 2 Aug. 1968

The Hotel in Amsterdam recalls on the surface the Noel Coward of
Design for Living and *Present Laughter*, with his showbiz ethic of
Bohemian self-reliance, comradely malice and loyalty to the freemason-
ry of craft. But there the overextended parallel between Osborne and
Coward ends, not before time. Osborne's new comedies, if you can call
them comedies at all, are infinitely sourer, more disillusioned and complex: less celebrations of an ideal show-business morality than studies in
its corruption, and the corruption of the England that Archie Rice saw as
a huge, crumbling old theatre.

His new plays bear an unobtrusive joint title: 'For the Meantime'
[this phrase was used in the advertising, but is not in the text or pro-

gramme — M.P.]. The double meaning is now obvious. Not only are these interim works, deliberately smaller in scope than *The Entertainer*, *Luther* or *Inadmissible Evidence*. They are also plays for a time that is mean, which permits nothing larger or more generous. All the good, brave causes are not merely dead, but rotten. The only guidance the creator of Jimmy Porter can offer the generation which made him its spokesman is these dual studies in survival: twin portraits of English heads just keeping their chins above a rising tide of bitchery and selfishness by bitching back, more loudly and self-assertively, first. . . .

In a sudden, short-storyish final twist, you discover that it's KL who depended on them, not they on him. The bitch-god was no god at all. The life they lead is the life they have chosen. Laurie's primacy is his honesty which refuses to let them forget they are damned, but he has used it none the less to lead them into damnation. It's a powerful, mature moral indictment, documented with a finely precise and detailed accuracy which should make the plays some day as invaluable to historians of the sixties as Thackeray to Victorian scholars and Scott Fitzgerald to students of the twenties. Cumulatively, along with *Inadmissible Evidence*, they add up to an impressive body of work, our most penetrating and truthful portrait gallery of the mean time we inhabit.

Ronald Bryden, 'Studies in Survival',
The Observer, 7 July 1968

The Right Prospectus

A play for television.
Transmitted: BBC-1, 22 Oct. 1970 (dir. Alan Cooke; with George Cole as Mr. Newbold and Elvi Hale as Mrs. Newbold).
Published: Faber, 1970.

A couple in early middle-age, the wife pregnant, are seen as pupils at a boys' boarding school. 'At no time does anyone, including staff or boys, seem aware of the age, sex or relation of the Newbolds. They are new boys.'

The idea for *The Right Prospectus* came to [Osborne] in a dream. 'I very often find ideas in dreams. This one is a very common experience — the adult who dreams he is back at school. People do hark back to their schooldays obsessively. '

Anne Chisholm, ' "Writing for Television is like
Writing Short Stories" ',
Radio Times, 17-23 Oct. 1970

It started with a splendid basic idea — a middle-aged couple decide to go back to Public School — after that it went absolutely nowhere and had absolutely nothing to say at considerable length.

Stanley Price, 'TV Drama', *Plays and Players*,
Dec. 1970, p. 59

On the level of nightmare it was perfect. The acceptance of a 45-year-old man and his wife as in no way incongruous by the boys or masters had just the right matter-of-fact horror to it, and there were those apparently absurd breaks in the logic (suddenly the two 'schoolboys' were eating a large meal with wine in a hotel) which, at the time, seem perfectly reasonable. As a dream the play worked, but as you'd expect Osborne didn't let it rest there. Into this vase he poured all his customary vices and virtues: his equivocal feelings about class, England, and sex; his marvellous rhetoric; his inability to prune. On this occasion his qualities were well in the lead and, as in most true works of art, there were so many levels that it was impossible to grasp all of them at one sitting. The high-spot in my view — one of those speeches which have the stamp of a major writer — was the lecture on the meaning of the House delivered by the cruel and beautiful head-boy to his subservient middle-aged fag. The balance between cynicism and conviction in this speech, its sexual puritanism expressed in language of coarse frankness, said a great deal about the exercise of power in our time. Dazzling. . . . Despite the fact that it was impossible not to recognize affinities with *If* [Lindsay Anderson film, 1968], I found that it was a more profound, less self-indulgent and finally an infinitely more satisfying exploration of the areas they examined in common.

George Melly, 'Back to Dream-School',
The Observer, 25 Oct. 1970

West of Suez

A play in two acts.
First London production: Royal Court Th., 17 Aug. 1971 (dir. Anthony

Page; with Ralph Richardson as Wyatt Gillman, Patricia Lawrence as Robin, Jill Bennett as Frederica, Sheila Ballantine as Evangie, Penelope Wilton as Mary, Geoffrey Palmer as Edward, and Nigel Hawthorne as Christopher), transferred to Cambridge Th., 6 Oct. 1971.
Published: Faber, 1971.

A villa on a Caribbean island, till recently a British colony. A retired brigadier and his wife, Robin, entertain her father, Wyatt Gillman, and her three sisters, two of them with husbands. Robin is in a second marriage, and has accepted the limited satisfactions of her life. Frederica, the second daughter, is sick, an insomniac, married to a pathologist who repeats that he is a 'blood and shit' man. Evangie, the third, is single and a would-be writer. Mary, the youngest and the only one with children, is married to a northern teacher and has partly withdrawn from her family. Wyatt, a famous writer and the main character, dislikes all the changes of his lifetime and asserts that 'Words alone are certain good'. The lawn is green and the sun hot, and they swim and drink. Wyatt gives an interview to a black woman reporter from the local paper, patronising her. A savage American student denounces them all as 'pigs', then black guerillas rush in and shoot Wyatt. The pathologist has the last line: 'My God — they've shot the fox'.

The play is about decaying of tongues, not just of colonial empires but of emotional empires, too.

Osborne, quoted in *Evening Standard*, 30 July 1971

What distinguishes this from Osborne's previous full-length work is that the main character is not absolutely dominant: he's but one contribution to an impressionistic sample of Britons left floundering and gasping by the 'winds of change' — aimless, bibulous, quarrelsome, sad, perhaps even doomed. Chekhov, you think; and the comparison is less than happy for Osborne. Perhaps he's ventured too far from mouthpieces, megaphones and strident ennui. Perhaps he just can't handle so many characters. Perhaps his sharp, aggressive dialogue is ill-suited to psychological subtlety and the undertow of relationship. As it is, much of the characterization seems merely abortive, and strong hints lead nowhere. . . . Nothing happens — and that, you feel, is the way Osborne prefers it.

A chair, a drink, and thou; an inconsequential conversation about old times: that is happiness. Indeed, his sympathies are most engaged when his people talk of ration books or public schools or trips to colonies or (God help us) the yellow-brown photos of yore. . . . Its basic tendency is to idealize the supposed decency, dignity and warmth of the imperial British. It is self-satisfied and more than a little chauvinistic.

Benedict Nightingale, 'Osborne's Old Times', *New Statesman,*
27 Aug. 1971, p. 277

Here is Osborne's *Heartbreak House* . . . and Wyatt Gillman is an inverted Shotover. Shaw, too, over fifty years ago, was concerned to pillory, with regret, a slow-pulsed, over-ripe civilization; but he was still able to set up against it a rampaging old mystic with his eyes on the stars, even though by that time he had almost lost any faith in human nature. Osborne's alchemy leaves us with a man whose potential talents have been wholly exercised in constructing ironical defences; behind them he passes the time in the role-playing of total scepticism.

Sir Ralph's portrait of this man, a burnt-out case from birth, seems to me a total triumph. The big frame moves with a puppet-like angularity, plays at a babyish physical incompetence. But the head turns like an old stag's, the eyes, widening and narrowing, are always watchful — and the voice takes on a score of colours just as the phrasing, the pauses, the downright breaks are themselves a miracle of characterization. False innocence brings in the hint of a whimper, calculated self-reproach a touch of unction; marvellously controlled, too, the voluble flood of embarrassment with which he greets his fellow-writer; and an absolute kaleidoscope, not without flashes of steel, colours his duel with the woman journalist.

J.W. Lambert, *Plays in Review, 1956-1980,*
ed. Gareth and Barbara Lloyd Evans (Batsford, 1985), p. 181-2,
from *Sunday Times,* 22 Aug. 1971

A potent, thoughtful and eminently entertaining evening in the theatre. Not that it is an easy play: much of it is still to be digested long after one leaves the auditorium, and the frames of reference within which it has been constructed are a curious amalgam of Chekhovian nostalgia, present despair and future terror. . . . Osborne's purpose . . . is to build a play for our uneasy time on the ground plans of earlier theatrical writers; not only Chekhov and Shaw but even Coward (in his *South Sea Bubble* mood) are invoked here like dramatic ghosts at a banquet, and the result is a densely packed, multi-levelled celebration of the void . . . a sardonic, almost bitchy realization that, as none of Osborne's predecessors had to accept or even realize, the emptiness is all. . . . *West of Suez* is, ultimately, Osborne's most depressing play; even the Colonel in *Look Back in Anger* had more going for him than is finally allowed Wyatt Gillman, suspended in time and space like an articulate scarecrow attempting to come to terms with the future even while it is killing him.

Sheridan Morley, *Review Copies* (Robson, 1974), p. 87-8

Instead of being a lament for the loss of empire, the play is really about the fate of western civilization. It is not a hymn to times past but a prophetic warning about times to come; not a piece of Tory nostalgia but a cry of liberal despair. It is true, of course, that Osborne sets the action in a former British colony that has recently gained its independence and that there is a good deal of talk about the vanished lifestyle of Empire. In one densely written passage the author-hero and his daughters simply catalogue some of the things they remember from their own family past: the fading photographs of amateur theatricals, the timetable of the South India railway, books scented with curry-powder. But this is no more than Osborne's own Proustian acknowledgment of the evocative power of insignificant objects (in *Time Present* old theatrical posters and bills spark off a similar total recall) and is even a mark of the characters' slightly self-indulgent sentimentality. For a genuine parallel to Osborne's attitude to our colonial past, one should look to James Ivory's film, *Shakespeare Wallah*, which shows a tumbledown theatrical troupe touring a changing, post-imperial India: like Ivory, Osborne admits the necessity of change but has a profound sympathy for people left stranded by the tide of history.

West of Suez, however, is not really about empire. It is about the break-up of any civilization that no longer puts its trust in reason, in respect for other people's values and, above all, in language. As has been pointed out, the play is built round a preoccupation with words. Three of the characters are writers; people are constantly commenting on the quality of each other's verbal style; and Jed, the American hippie who finally savages the bourgeois-decadents, is shown to have a pathetically limited capacity for invective. As a writer, Osborne clearly has a vested interest in language and its careful preservation; but what he says in the play is that if you don't believe in language you are not only sacrificing something of your own essential selfhood but you are also destroying a bridge between human beings and hastening the day when the law of the jungle prevails. . . .

His plays catch and interpret the mood of a time; and in *West of Suez* he is (I believe) alerting us to the fact that there is a strong fascist instinct currently abroad. It is rather like Gorki's *Enemies* seen from another angle: the difference here is that the beleaguered bourgeoisie are threatened not by rising social and political progress but by a spirit of fanatical intolerance.

Michael Billington, 'Osborne Wallah',
The Guardian, 7 Oct. 1971

Wyatt Gilman says that what he is afraid of is not death, but ludicrous death, and that he feels that this death is in the air. Almost immediately afterwards the death comes: violent, inexorable, and absurd, a thing both to be desired and to weep over in rebellion and shame. This powerful and troubling ambivalence of feeling Mr. Osborne conveys in as reverberating a last line as you will hear in any theatre, a line that brings to a fitting conclusion one of his finest works. It is a line that in not more than a dozen words creates in our minds a vision of that English countryside which once seemed eternal, its beauty and its courage, but also in its inexplicable, indefensible conventions, and its ruthlessness. Possibly Mr. Osborne despairs too soon, but the splendour of his despair cannot be denied. Neither can the wit and the theatrical effectiveness of his play.

Harold Hobson, 'Empire at Sunset',
Sunday Times, 10 Oct. 1971

Wyatt Gillman is killed, caught in the crossfire. Curtain. So what? Death of a symbol? An irrelevance getting in the way? If so, the play is a massive demonstration of its own failure, for it lingers nostalgically over the way of life it declares redundant, and few of the main characters are seen, anyway, in relation to their 'real' environment. Of the alternatives we glimpse only that futile stereotype of an eternal student, and broad, retreating black backs. What has the hippy been saying to Edward, always out of the audience's and Frederica's earshot? Why does the domiciled American lollop morosely about like the loose-end of plot he is? Why does Osborne put so many of his personal dislikes — of critics, needless to say, as well as tourists — into the mouth of a character with whom he does not, presumably, wish to be identified, at the very moment when that character, between and sometimes along the lines of his interview, comes nearest to stating his credo? And couldn't a less clumsy way have been found for him to do it, anyway? Lots more questions — mostly peripheral to what the play may or may not be 'about'. For it doesn't usefully provoke: it merely irritates.

Simon Trussler, 'Demonstration of Failure', *Tribune*, 3 Sept. 1971

Hedda Gabler

A play in four acts, 'adapted' from the play by Henrik Ibsen.

First London production: Royal Court Th., 28 June 1972 (dir. Anthony
   Page; with Jill Bennett as Hedda Gabler, Ronald Hines as Tesman,
   Denholm Elliott as Brack, Barbara Ferris as Mrs. Elvsted, and Brian
   Cox as Lovborg).

Televised: ITV (Yorkshire), 3 Mar. 1981, cut to 90 mins. (with Diana
   Rigg as Hedda Gabler, Denis Lill as Tesman, Alan Dobie as Brack,
   Elizabeth Bell as Mrs. Elvstead, and Philip Bond as Lovborg).

Published: Faber, 1972.

I have been fascinated for a long time by *Hedda Gabler.* By this, I don't
mean merely the character, but the play itself. For, like most great plays,
the apparent central character exists only by the favour of the other characters in the play, however small. . . . Her tragedy, if it can be called one,
is that of being born *bored* and that is what is fascinating about her in
the annals of dramatic literature. The very concept was unique at the
time. She is a loser, whereas Mrs. Elvsted is an odds-on favourite. The
important point about the adaptation and production of the play is very
simple: the complexity of the character of Hedda Gabler is richer only if
the other characters in the play are also seen to be made as rich as they
are. They are all, by any standards, a pretty shabby lot. Hedda is a born
victim but she does have the gift of energy, while Mrs. Elvsted is a very
cold cookie indeed.

Osborne, 'Introduction', p. 7-8

[*Hedda Gabler*] is billed as an adaptation by John Osborne, but it's not
at all easy to make out where, aside from at the most superficial level,
the adapting has been done. It's not a matter of dialogue, for Osborne has
made no substantial alterations in this area, except to update the idiom
slightly, which is the sort of thing any translator of Ibsen might reason-
ably do. And apart fom one or two faintly meretricious touches, like
Hedda's hint of a lesbian penchant for Mrs. Elvsted, the characters
remain very much as Ibsen conceived them.

Derek Mahon, *The Listener,* 6 July 1972

[Osborne] has not imposed himself on *Hedda Gabler.* He shows that
there is something in *Hedda Gabler* that has imposed itself on him, and
the evening becomes an absorbing demonstration of what that something
is. It is a perception of boredom as one of the most powerful activating

forces in human nature. Hedda is the representative of an upper class which has lost its function in existence, but not its vitality.

Harold Hobson, *Sunday Times*, 2 July 1972

[Diana Rigg is] an apt choice to play Hedda Gabler, the protean woman trapped into destruction by her times, her class, her character and her beauty, all together in effect, being an unplayable hand. But as suits in cards, these four factors must be used to make any version of Ibsen's play work. Misanthropy and misogyny vie, in much of John Osborne's work; and so, in this adaptation by him, the aspect of Hedda which shows her as an object — an object of male adoration, longing, lust — and so preoccupied with experiments with men's souls, is underscored. But, because indications of the society she lives in are rendered cursory, there is no sense of the inevitability of her actions: she appears to be a bitch, and Hedda is not merely a bitch. The Osborne version, chopped in half from the original for ITV, has turned Ibsen's tragedy into a study in cynicism.

Geoffrey Cannon, *Sunday Times*, 26 Feb. 1981

A Sense of Detachment

A play in two acts.
First London production: Royal Court Th., 4 Dec. 1972 (dir. Frank Dunlop; with Rachel Kempson as Older Lady, Nigel Hawthorne as Chairman, and John Standing as Chap).
Published: Faber, 1973; with *A Patriot for Me*, 1983.

Osborne has opted for a freewheeling style of anti-theatre, which has been interpreted by some as a symptom of despair with contemporary life (including the theatre), but which came across to me as a rather happy, slightly self-indulgent party game: a Christmas charade, perhaps? We are in limbo. There is no story and no shape. Six characters [Chairman, Chap, Girl, Older Lady, Father, Grandfather] (!), stereotyped and unnamed, occupy the stage, react on each other (mostly abusively), and deplore the fact that 'everything has been done'. I know that feeling well. He extends his piece to a third dimension, by using a beer-swilling football supporter in a box . . . and an ordinary bloke, complete with lady wife, who interrupts the dialogue and goes for periodic visits to the bar. The second half turns into a personal anthology of Osborne favourites: excerpts of classical music, old songs and dances, snippets of poetry and prose, and film projections of paintings. . . . Towards the end, a pulpit is wheeled on, and one by one the characters deliver little sermons on a variety of topics, including Ireland, Women's Lib., and, finally and most movingly, a paean for the Eternal Feminine and the miracle of falling in love. There is nothing despicable in this and Osborne is always worth hearing. Whether it would have been wiser to hold this examination of the rudiments of his craft and stock-taking of his ideas in private rather than in public is open to argument. . . . Rachel Kempson, looking ineffably English, read courageously from a sales catalogue of pornography the most explicitly-worded accounts of sexual perversions yet uttered on the London stage, thus driving a large number of shocked theatregoers to the exits.

Frank Marcus, 'Shades of Night',
Sunday Telegraph, 10 Dec. 1972, p. 18

There are in my view some superb moments in the latest Osborne, be it the vision of a land of hope and glory turned into a land of hopeful Tories or that of Hugh Hastings at the piano, the embodiment of Thirties Man and in a way a lynchpin of Osborne's thesis since he represents the world we have left, still offering with pathetic eagerness to do a 'a passable imitation of Melville Gideon'. 'We do not love, eat or cherish' is one of the play's conclusions, 'we now merely exchange'; for that alone, it seems to me, the play needs to be considered as something more than a reactionary load of old cobblers.

Sheridan Morley, *Review Copies*, p. 157-9

You might look at the piece as a terminal point of Osborne's derision which has now spread from the world outside to the theatrical process itself. Everything has been done; everything is boring, except perhaps memories of old times and good prose; and nothing new is worth doing for those fools out front anyway. . . . Finally a somewhat baroque message is delivered by Mr. Standing and Denise Coffey. It seems to be to the effect that technology and going into Europe make it harder for people to fall in love.

Irving Wardle, 'Unnamed Figures in a Limbo Scene',
The Times, 5 Dec. 1972, p. 14

The word 'detachment' is the key to the production. The author is detached from the actors, for whom he supplies no roles: the actors are detached from the audience, for whom they offer condescending snips of old routines: and they are all alienated from the surrounding culture.

John Elsom, 'Supporting Stoke', The Listener, 14 Dec. 1972

Osborne has chosen the occasion to get a few beefs off his chest about the present condition of the dramatic art, with particular attention to Harold Pinter and Samuel Beckett. I have a fair amount of sympathy with this point of view — and it is engaging to have it stated at the Royal Court, of all places — but I'm afraid Osborne has not quite mastered the trick of writing about bores and boredom without being ineffably boring himself. I'm sorry to say, too, that he runs into a similar difficulty in ventilating his severe opinion of the debasement of language as it applies especially to matters of love and sex.

Kenneth Hurren, 'Osborne and Arden',
The Spectator, 9 Dec 1972, p. 934

A Place Calling Itself Rome

Play in two acts, adaptation of Shakespeare's *Coriolanus*.
Unperformed.
Published: Faber, 1973

Obviously Rome could have called itself London or Moscow or Noa-Noa for Osborne's purposes, and the play would have been better if Rome had not been used. For the story of Rome's one-time hero who is expelled by the people and returns leading an army to sack the city is in no way improved by its half-hearted allegiance to Shakespeare's version. It would need more than police in flak jackets and helicopters to convert *Coriolanus* into modern terms. Osborne would have to rework the entire story into a truly modern idiom, submerging Shakespeare in his own voice.

He can't resist Shakespeare's structure, or at times his language, though he seems fully capable of resisting Shakespeare's humanist judgment of the people of Rome and Coriolanus. In fact, the chief non-Shakespearean contributions to the story seem to be a heating-up of the insults Coriolanus hurls at the people and a general degradation of the Roman populace. Where Shakespeare calls the Roman people 'Citizens', Osborne designates them as 'Mob'; exactly where Shakespeare has

Coriolanus say, 'Hence, old goat!', Osborne makes him say, 'Go on, get them together "policeman" — policeman of the piss poor! Get off out of it, hairy charm-pits.' And the modern Mob is no random gathering but a collection of types: 'students, fixers, pushers, policemen, unidentifiable public, obvious trade unionists, journalists and the odd news camera team, sound men, etc.', sporting banners which read, 'Caius Marcius: Go Fuck Yourself' and 'No More Trix Just a Fix'.

In spite of the heavy anti-mob bias of the play, its politics are even vaguer than Shakespeare's, largely because the new Coriolanus is more arrogant, more prideful and less heroic than Shakespeare's.

'Damn You, and You, and You', *Times Literary Supplement,*
4 Jan. 1974, p. 14

This angry, superior young man, with an awful mother, was obviously congenial to Osborne. . . . The adaptation, if we compare scene by scene, is fairly straightforward. The title — *A Place Calling Itself Rome* — suggests that we may apply the lesons wherever they fit and is in many ways more suitable for Shakespeare's version. *Coriolanus* is first and foremost about Rome, whereas Osborne's version looks more deeply into the personality of the hero. Thus Osborne invents a first scene in the bedroom of Coriolanus as he dreams.

Arnold Hinchliffe, *John Osborne*, p. 118

Ms, or Jill and Jack

A play for television: 30 minutes.
Transmitted: ITV (Yorkshire), 11 Sept. 1974 (dir. Mike Newell; with Jill Bennett as Jill and John Standing as Jack).
Published: with *The End of Me Old Cigar*, Faber, 1975.

The play's kinship was with the Wildean epigram which achieves wit by the simple inversion of a banal proposition. Thus 'Work is the curse of the drinking classes', thus Jill and Jack, which showed us a sophisticated, chauffeur-driven executive out on a date (dinner at 'my club') with a pouty bit of goods from the suburbs.

It was all much as you would expect, except that it was a wickedly comic gem because the executive was played by Jill Bennett and the pouty bit of goods by John Standing. Jill's club, of course, featured old ladies snoring in leather chairs. 'I hope it won't be too stuffy for you', she says, while Jack has a little sulk about what the rain has done to his hair: 'It cost me two quid and what about my jacket?' At dinner Jill tries to bring him round, her foot finding his under cover of the table, and afterwards she leaves him sheltering in the doorway while she charges into a cloudburst to fetch the Rolls. At home, a bachelor dream-pad designed by Roger Andrews, she fails to get him into bed by playing the wrong card: 'I never expected you to bring up marriage', says Jack. . . . Its beauty lay in masterly detail, in the writing and the acting, which commented wittily on the minutiae of a thousand telly plays where Jack makes the running.

Tom Stoppard,
The Observer, 15 Sept. 1974

Bennett's Jill was as masterful and disarming as Ronald Colman at his best; but Mr. Standing had the better part and his vain, petulant and faintly crumpled Jack sailed clear of all poovery to project a wholly plausible and extremely funny picture of the weaker sex. . . . Sexual warfare remains John Osborne's primary source of invention, and few playwrights have fought it over so variegated a field. He is unrivalled, save perhaps by Amis and Albee, in the vitality with which he invests the figure of the male bitch *(Hotel in Amsterdam)*; much less successful, but no less in thrall to the mannish lady *(A Patriot for Me)*; in *West of Suez* he matched these two figures for the first time in the marvellous duologue of a wife who could only attack and a husband who defended himself with every mean trick in the book. *Ms, or Jill and Jack* was slighter than any of these.

Michael Ratcliffe, 'John Osborne at His Coolest',
The Times, 12 Sept. 1974

The Gift of Friendship

A play for television.
Transmitted: ITV (Yorkshire), 24 Sept. 1974 (dir. Mike Newell; with Alec Guinness as Jocelyn, Michael Gough as Bill, and Sarah Badel as Madge).
Published: Faber, 1972.

Jocelyn, an eccentric elderly novelist, living in affluence in a

country house, summons Bill, another novelist and old acquain-
tance, to visit him for dinner. Though they dislike each other,
Jocelyn asks his guest to be his literary executor. He dies soon
after (suicide?), leaving Bill reading diaries and puzzling over
the relationship.

There can be no doubt that Mr. Osborne bore a number of Evelyn
Waugh's particular circumstances in mind when composing the figure of
Jocelyn Broome. . . . There was some confusing stuff about the seven
deadly sins and some precipitate cutting but these did nothing to obscure
the main theme, which rang out murderously clear: that all writers,
forced to ignore the present and future in order to batten on the past, are
utterly alone; or the secondary one, that England has been destroyed out
of sheer stupidity and idleness. 'I think we're giving away a lot, don't
you?' remarked Jocelyn over the after-dinner port, and Wakely agreed
with a suitably long face. The grimmest irony of all was that, since they
were both merely writers, there wasn't a thing that either of them was
going to do about it.

Michael Ratcliffe, *The Times*, 25 Sept. 1974

The kind of play which slices off your self-confidence at the knee-caps
and cuts you down to size. 'Did I,' you wonder wildly, 'did I drop off
halfway and miss some key scene? There was a key. I do remember that.
The Great Writer kept putting it in books with enigmatic inscriptions.'
Perhaps if I heard it all over again and slowly. I do not, however, think it
possible to do *The Gift of Friendship* more slowly than it was done on
Tuesday. A wife would say something like 'Do you feel well?' 'Well.'
The husband would shout, biting through his bottom lip. 'Of course I'm
well.' The wife would then look stricken, the cream caramel would
shudder, the butler would stiffen. You just knew that the full freight and
weight of the exchange had somehow escaped you. Fool and dolt that
you must be. Innumerate imbecile to keep counting confusedly on your
fingers when people talked about the eighth deadly sin. It was a reason-
ably convincing portrait of a tormented Evelyn Waugh figure. And there
was an excellently excruciating meal. The sort that are so familiar to
viewers of television plays and which amply account in themselves for
the popularity of the television snack. It was a play so concerned about
the labour of language, working with words, being true to that trade that
it should perhaps have been a short story which would have given you
time to turn back and try again.

Nancy Banks-Smith, *The Guardian*, 25 Sept. 1974

71

Osborne chose the treacherous theme of writers' relationships to their work and to each other. Treacherous because it so often gives rise to the kind of professional narcissism to which the viewer can be legitimately indifferent. But largely because of the finely-tooled dialogue and sure-footed gradual revelation of character and background, as the despised Wakely, editor and writer, prepared to respond to what amounts to a summons to dinner from Jocelyn Broome, the celebrated writer, the relationship held our interest. Broome is a cold, self-critical creature who affirms that one can be close to death and close to God but not to people. He has given his life a 'long, wasting appraisal'; discovered himself to have become 'overblown, covetous, full of smug foreboding', and he is planning to vindictively appoint his guest, who figures contemptuously in his diaries, as his literary executor. Osborne catches well the ashen flavour of writers at a stage when they have become convinced that their 'seam has run dry' and that their efforts have perhaps been nothing more than a morbid exercise. Their women, Leueen MacGrath as Broome's fatigued and uncomprehending wife and Sarah Badel as Wakely's resentful third wife, reinforce the sense of defeat and decay which surround their men. . . . Allowing his chief character to lament bitterly that 'we did have the finest language in the world', Osborne himself here displays a not inconsiderable ability to mine and refine a telling word and phrase.

Peter Lennon, 'Success Stories',
Sunday Times, 29 Sept. 1974, p. 38

The End of Me Old Cigar

A play in two acts.
First London production: Greenwich Th., 16 Jan. 1975 (dir. Max
  Stafford-Clark; with Rachel Roberts as Lady Regine Frimley, Jill
  Bennett as Isobel Sands, and Keith Barron as Leonard Grimthorpe).
Published: with *Jill and Jack*, Faber, 1975.

It's the title of an old music-hall song which was a great favourite of Harry Champion's. You, I hope, will see why it is called that when you see the play. It's a comedy. At least I think it's a comedy and other people think it hasn't got a funny line in it. I think of myself as a very comic writer.

Osborne, quoted by Mark Amory, 'Jester Flees the Court',
Sunday Times Magazine, 24 Nov. 1974, p. 34

The End of Me Old Cigar sets out as one thing and ends as another. It begins very much as a Restoration satire. A confederacy of women plot to end male domination at a stroke. Their object is to catch a sufficiently large, representative, and influential sample of them with their trousers down and reveal to the world a two-way mirror's eye-view of their corruptibility, decadence and unfitness to rule. The organizing genius is a Hackney girl now fortunate enough to have made herself Lady Regine Frimley, who madames a house of pleasure for Men that Matter. Millionaires are welcome, MPs and top pop singers only marginally less so. The bait for the night of triumph Osborne promises to show us is a wide selection of Women's Libbers including housewife, painted Lady and American feminist stormtrooper who enter the scene heralded by a thumbnail sketch and likely potential as assessed by Lady Regine and the woman she's chosen as her key ally and conspirator, Stella Shrift (Sheila Ballantine), a bitchy gossip columnist. The principal oversight in the elaborate plans which go into details of who is going to whisk whom into which bedroom, is that the person responsible for filming the night's proceedings is a man. Should he not deliver the goods, it's all a useless exercise. However, the stage is filled with the various arrivals, and we're all set for orgy and revolution in the second act. But Osborne ducks out of the problem he has set himself. He ditches the satirical framework he's built up, axes characters who've only just stuck their noses in and replaces it all with a little bedchamber-verité love scene between Keith Barron and Jill Bennett. Osborne then finishes the play with a haste that suggests either loss of interest or a need to take his typewriter in for servicing. A core of simple truth and love is enough to stop the nation — for Lady Regine's super-brothel is as much the nation as Jimmy Porter's flat — from falling into utter decadence and consequent revolution; that seems to be the thinking. The love scene itself is strangely unsatisfactory. The two seem improbable guests at this particular feast. . . . Max Stafford-Clark, who directs, seems to be at a loss as to how to handle the switch between the two halves of the play. Understandably. But never let the ability of Osborne to thrill an audience be underestimated. He can always produce moments when a character soars into voice with a speed, fluency and mounting gusto that fair catches the breath. It happens here in Rachel Roberts's tirade against masculinity which she crackles round the theatre.

Ivan Howlett, *Plays and Players*, Mar. 1975, p. 28-9

All [Act 1], with its backbiting wit, and its recklessness with reputations, is a *School for Scandal* liberated into the sexual licence of the present day. . . . Nothing so carefully prepared in the first act ever comes at all. What happens in the second is quite different. . . . This salvation, this tiny thing in England that is still valuable in Mr. Osborne's eyes, is manifested in the fresh, innocent coolness of Jill Bennett's performance as the most unexpected of the call-girls, and in one of those old music-hall songs for which Mr. Osborne has such affection. There is in the finely conceived play a gleam of hope.

Harold Hobson, 'A Patriot for Me', *Sunday Times*,
19 Jan. 1975, p. 37

The couple who meet at the country-house orgy admit charmingly and openly that they are not very good at 'it'. The result is that they are, and this makes them blissfully happy. So, sexual honesty is added to friendship, integrity, and the correct use of the English language (unpolluted by jargon), to those facets of modern life which Osborne considers worth cherishing. Like Schnitzler in *La Ronde*, he uses the revelation of true identity at moments of sexual intimacy in order to dissect and demolish the pretensions and hypocrisies of a decaying society. . . . If only he had taken more trouble over it, this might have been his *Heartbreak House*. Unfortunately, it is developed very perfunctorily. . . . This, then, is not at all a well-made play. It just so happened that I liked it enormously.

Frank Marcus, 'The Story of Mr. O.', *Sunday Telegraph*,
26 Jan. 1975, p. 16

The Picture of Dorian Gray

Play in three acts, 'adapted from the novel by Oscar Wilde'.
First production: Greenwich Th., London, 13 Feb. 1975 (dir. Clive Donner; with Michael Kitchen as Dorian Gray, Anton Rodgers as Lord Henry Wotton, and John McEnery as Basil).
Television: BBC-1, 'Play of the Month', 19 Sept. 1976 (dir. John Gorrie; with Perter Firth as Dorian Gray, John Gielgud as Henry Wotton, and Jeremy Brett as Basil).
Published: Faber, 1973.

I have called it simply but deliberately 'A Moral Entertainment' because that is what it is. The original is a superb entertainment; notwithstanding all the things that one knows about it and have been said so many times. It is, of course, melodramatic and steeped in the personal but painful yillery-yallery of Wilde himself. . . . *The Picture of Dorian Gray* is not only a remarkable achievement of its time, given all its faults, but the germinal story is an inspired one like, say, that of Jekyll and Hyde. . . .

One of the things that has struck me about the original book is its feeling of wilful courage and despair, the two qualities only too clearly embodied in the spirit of Wilde himself. It is an infuriating work, often misleading, sometimes deadly serious when it should be self-mocking, and so on. For example, there was a time some years ago when the ethic of effortless physical beauty might have seemed no more than a camp, tiresomely self-abusing piece of attitudinizing. But today? What are the things most valued, sought after? Beauty, yes; youth, most certainly. Youth has become, like death, almost a taboo subject. Everyone is not merely afraid of losing it but of even admitting that such a possibility exists. Again, youth is all important, all reaching, all powerful. It is obligatory to be trim, slim, careless. The lines of age on Dorian Gray's portrait are a very modern likeness in all this. . . .

So then, we enter into a world which is without a sense of sin but acutely aware of something vague but daily threatening which might even still be called evil; like the present interest in occult sciences and astrology, for instance, it is a world in which the truth of opposites is clear, if not always understood; where duality is usefully all.

'Introduction', *The Picture of Dorian Gray*, p. 11-15

[Osborne] has tampered little with the melodramatic story of the beautiful young man whose face and form remain untouched by time while the painted features in his portrait sinisterly reflected the ever-deepening corruption of his daily life through the years. The chief delight in this play, as in the book, is the ineffable Lord Henry Wotton, borne on a languid tide of epigrams through the world of fashionable drawing-rooms, clubs and galleries, always in perfect control of himself and everything around him, ever ready to turn a phrase (but never, of course, a hair) whatever the circumstances. . . . The Osborne version is itself compact of style and wit, and surely quite a lot of the splendidly ornate pronouncements are all his own work, the very occasional anachronistic word serving to add zest to the paradox rather than to decrease the flavour of the *mot*. Some of the later lurid twists are perhaps less effective than the earlier polished toying with the theme.

Romilly Cavan, 'Scripts', *Plays and Players*, Jan. 1974, p. 65

I saw a respectful rendering of the original, amounting in theatrical terms to no more than a hollow piece of Grand Guignol. The first half was sluggish; thereafter the story began to grip and the director, Clive Donner, used all available resources of light and sound to create ghostly and lurid climaxes. The inadequacy of Michael Kitchen in the name-part was not entirely the actor's fault. Dorian, like Wedekind's Lulu, is the object rather than the subject of the play: his face is a blank mirror, reflecting other people's ideals. . . . By and large, the words stuck obstinately to the printed page. The result was not particularly entertaining.

Frank Marcus, 'Red Shadow', *Sunday Telegraph*, 16 Feb. 1975, p. 14

Faced with the challenge of telescoping *Dorian Gray* . . . Osborne hit upon a novel and ingenious procedure: he took a bit from the beginning and he took a bit from the end. We stay close to Wilde, in *Digest* form, until the suicide of Sybil Vane, with Dorian being sullen, callous, lordly; we then move on, if you please, to the murder of Basil — with Dorian a cackling blackguard. What then could have happened to the lad? Well, two decades of rarefied debauchery, if you know your Wilde, but only an indeterminate bout of profligacy, if you trust your Osborne. 'My dear boy, I haven't seen you for weeks', says John Gielgud as Lord Henry, who has been off-screen for 18 years (and who must have been very confused anyway, since he is 40 years too old for the part). . . . The heart of the story — which is the story of Dorian's corruption — is the section Osborne omits: the section that begins with Lord Henry's loan of the decadent French novel ('Dorian Gray had been poisoned by a book', says Wilde flatly) and goes on to explore his sick infatuation with 'the luxury of the dead.' . . . If Wilde had thought the idea dramatic, he would doubtless have been the first to write a play about it.

Martin Amis, *New Statesman*, 24 Sept. 1976, p. 427-8

Watch It Come Down

A play in two acts.
First London production: Old Vic Th., 24 Feb. 1976 (dir. Bill Bryden;
with Jill Bennett as Sally, Frank Finlay as Ben, Michael Feast as
Raymond, Michael Gough as Glen, and Susan Fleetwood as Jo),
transferred to Lyttelton Th., 20 Mar. 1976.
Published: Faber, 1975.

Set in a country railway-station, converted as a house. Ben, a film director, and Sally, his wife, are middle-aged, bored and apathetic, and may separate. They exchange insults, drink a great deal, fight violently at the end of the first act. Offsage upstairs is an unwanted old mother. There is little to do: the man has been to London, had lunch with his young daughter and slept with his first wife; the woman twice goes out for country walks. Glen represents the older generation, a writer who completes three years' work on a biography and then dies. There are three younger people. Raymond is an amiable homosexual, who cooks and runs errands. Shirley, Sally's sister, paints badly and is mocked for being a protester. Jo paints too, loves Sally and the old man, and kills herself after he dies. The end comes suddenly with gun-fire. Ben, at the doorway, is shot and apparently killed, with a mention of local yobbos who dislike the different lifestyle at the station. Flashes and bullet-holes appear in the walls. The title refers to Glen quoting a sign he has seen: 'We demolish it: you watch it come down.'

As usual [the characters] consist of middle-aged art community emigres who seem to expend most of their creative energies in sexual warfare. There is the usual ambiguous treatment of homosexuality, and the usual see-saw betwee sabre-toothed insult and exchanges of childlike affections. And there is the usual assumption that these people, who still put their dwindling trust in personal relationships and the power of words, are among the last survivors of our dying civilization, shortly to be sacked by barbarous media men and land speculators brandishing the big lead ball. *Watch it Come Down* differs from its predecessors mainly in the degree of hysteria with which these points are restated; and in the feeling that perhaps human beings, however friendly, are simply too lethal to live close together without tearing one another to pieces.

Irving Wardle, *The Times*, 25 Feb. 1976

[A] comparison might be *Hay Fever*, rewritten by a strangely grouchy, woozy Coward. With their loud and public bickering, their determination to involve their guests in their private dramas, the couple played by Finlay and Bennett emerge as updated Blisses — more unattractive, more cantankerous, and at least as superficial. Indeed, the play confirms my suspicion that Osborne no longer has the objectivity, empathy or insight to create anything resembling a rounded, or even half-rounded, human being.

Benedict Nightingale, *New Statesman*, 5 Mar. 1976, p. 299

Watch it Come Down is another attempt to re-write *Heartbreak House*: a study of a doomed, fractious intelligentsia undermined both by its own sense of futility and by a collapsing society. But whereas Shaw, as befits an Irish playwright, managed to put more of England on to the stage than one would have thought possible, Osborne concentrates on such a thin, narrow strip of society that his apocalyptic finale lacks resonance.

The play shows all Osborne's talent for casual insult and for probing the scars and sores of a bad marriage. . . . The problem is Osborne's own attitude to this bizarre commune seems to waver. He admires the gift of friendship: yet he shows it dwindling into maudlin insularity. . . . Osborne is fatally torn between contempt for this inbred, sickly household and a pained admiration for their ability to parade their bleeding hearts. And this contributes not so much to a rich ambiguity as to a sense of theatrical confusion. . . . The play is an infuriating blend of the best and worst of Osborne: on the one hand, full of bilious wit (particularly about the English countryside) and shameless emotion and on the other technically gauche (one death, one suicide and one serious injury in the last five minutes) and intellectually muddled.

Michael Billington, *The Guardian*, 25 Feb. 1976

Almost a Vision

A play for television, 30 minutes.
Transmitted: ITV (Yorkshire), 'Wednesday Special', 1 Sept. 1976 (with Jill Bennett and Keith Barron).
Unpublished.

Osborne's preoccupation was not so much with the idea of romantic love, but with straightforward sex. After a quiet opening, the rest of the play was taken up with a dialogue between a man and a woman as, helped by champagne, they overcame their nervousness at the thought of sleeping together. As we know from his stage plays, Osborne has a very acute ear for the rhythms of everyday speech, and the often inconsequential remarks, pauses and occasional more profound statements were a joy to listen to, and often very funny. The two swapped ideas like tennis players warily getting to know each other's game at the beginning of the match, and this similarity was further enforced by the quick succession of close-ups of the actors' faces, as they revelled in the superb writing. . . . Peter Caldwell's fussy country-house bedroom set enforced the claustrophobic atmosphere.

Jackie Dyason, 'Two Original and Thoughtful Plays',
The Stage, 9 Sept. 1976, p. 15

Try a Little Tenderness

A play for television.
Unperformed.
Published: with *You're Not Watching Me, Mummy*, Faber, 1978.

A big pop festival is about to be held in a village, and the local upper middle class are uneasy. Ted Shilling, a bohemian novelist, gives them a plan for disrupting it. The second half focuses on Ted, his bored and unhappy wife, his deaf ex-Far East mother-in-law, his wife's bored friend, his rivalry for his son's girl friend, and the squatters occupying half his house. Ends with 'Struggles and mass panic as the different elements swirl about amongst each other. Horses, dogs, foxes, sheep, foxhounds, tractors, bulldozers, police vans, police dogs, loudspeakers, tents, toilets, stalls, makeshift huts, stands. Vicious climax. It is indeed like a battlefield by now'.

You're Not Watching Me, Mummy

A play for television.
Transmitted: ITV (Yorkshire), 20 Jan. 1980 (dir. James Ormerod; with Anna Massey as Jemima, Peter Sallis as Leslie, Gillian Martell as Mrs. Colbourne, and Suzanne Bertish as Lena).
Published: with *Try a Little Tenderness*, Faber, 1978.

Osborne, through Massey, presents the meaninglessness of a life lived for applause. His actress is one of those modern grandes *dames who must always be attended by homosexual acolytes. Massey and her dresser (nicely played by Peter Sallis) assault each other with lashings of abuse but the relationship is one of desperate mutual need. As the (improbably sumptuous) dressing room fills with unwelcome gawpers . . . the exhausted star creeps off to bed, the outsiders' insensitive inanities ringing in her ears. . . . The characters, drawn from a wide cross-section of society, do not, on the whole, understand one another.*

Contemporary Britain is despatched by means of jaundiced generalizations delivered on behalf of the author. There is an underlying thread of pathos. The plot is of the slimmest.
                              Michael Church, *The Times*, 19 Jan. 1980

Very Like a Whale

A play for television: 95 mins.
Transmitted: ITV (ATV), 13 Feb. 1980 (dir. Alan Bridges; with Alan
    Bates as Sir Jock and Gemma Jones as Lady Mellor).
Published: Faber, 1971.

Sir Jock Mellor, aged 47, a captain of industry, lives in the padded cell of a luxury life. He travels in cars so big no one touches, sleeps in beds so wide there is no contact. Through the windows of the Rolls he observes the exotic brutality of London by night. Secretaries and chauffeurs cocoon him at work; servants and a lonely wife shelter him at home. Everything money can buy is his and it's worthless. In a lifestyle abounding in choices he has no freedom. John Osborne's play tells in a straightforward manner of this man's last days. Triggered by the accolade of a knighthood and the hollow sham of its celebratory party, he tries belatedly to revive true closeness with those he knows. His wife, neglected for too long, bored and aimless, can only snipe back. The rising crescendo of their rows is one of the most painful sequences I can remember in television drama. . . . Sir Jock visits his aging father, Leslie Sands, cosy with his dog and telly, who ignores the attempted tenderness of his son's parting kiss. He visits a school friend painter and finds him polite but self-sufficient, calls on a doctor who is professionally friendly, looks up a former wife too eager to renew her hold, a son keen to escape. They all fail him and he stares his own failure in the face. We see little and learn less of where his working life has failed him, too. The play is about money and success, the ambition to have them and the assumption they are life's crowning glory. These are false gods. Glutted with objects, our lives have no substance. . . . We have a glossy and expensive play; mirrors, crystal, gleaming surfaces, Concorde, private hospitals, lavish gowns, cut roses.

Joan Bakewell, *The Times*, 14 Feb. 1980, p. 13

God Rot Tunbridge Wells

Dramatized documentary about Handel for television.
Transmitted: Channel 4, 6 Apr. 1985 (dir. Tony Palmer; with
Dave Griffiths as young Handel, and Trevor Howard as Old Handel).
Published: Handel's 14-page death-bed monologue, with *A Better Class of Person*, Faber, 1985.

[Handel dies a week after a dreadful performance of *The Messiah* by Tunbridge Wells Amateur Music Club: hence the title.]

It was certainly a 'flawed work' as they say. . . . The result, if a bit over-energetic and robust for some maidenly tastes, patently displayed our shared admiration for a God-given, devout and joyful worshipper of life itself. The reviews were almost uniformly dismissive if not hostile. The Old Buck still seemed hedged in by Victorian pieties from undevout journalists.

Osborne, 'Diary', *The Spectator*, 13 July 1985, p. 7

Handel, about whose love-life almost nothing is known, becomes a figure out of Henry Fielding, a musical Tom Jones, a young buck who roisters his way through respectable society, leching and duelling and exploiting the absurd public fads for opera, oratorio and whatever. . . . Palmer's Handel film is a vile travesty, patronizing Handel's period with comic Chaplinesque riots, and at 140 minutes a lengthy reminder only of Osborne's maudlin egotism. . . . What I cannot forgive is the portrait of Handel as a jumped-up opportunistic philistine remembering his time in Hamburg (quite well documented in fact) with the typical Osborne phrase, 'Italian opera snoring its way into our life'.

Tom Sutcliffe, 'Handel without Care',
The Guardian, 8 Apr. 1985, p. 7

Autobiography

A Better Class of Person. Faber, 1981; Penguin, 1982. [His autobiography to 1955].

Dramatised Version:
'An Extract of Autobiography for Television': 120 mins.
Transmitted: ITV (Thames), 1 July 1985 (dir. Frank Cvitanovich; with Eileen Atkins as Mrs. Osborne, and Alan Howard as Mr. Osborne).
Published: with *God Rot Tunbridge Wells,* Faber, 1985.

Against a war-time background, Osborne re-creates the bitter domestic battles that raged throughout his childhood. As his venerated father, a bookish consumptive, patiently wastes away, his execrated mother ferociously spits out resentment and rancour. Even bereavement fails to muffle her malevolence: 'This room'll 'ave to be fumigated', she moans as her husband's corpse is laid out. . . . Eileen Atkins's horror-comic performance, all pinched mouth and nipped waist, does justice to the whingeing truculence of this lipsticked misery: even reading a newspaper — pages turned in a flurry of crackling disturbance — becomes an act of aggression. But she adds depth and conviction, allowing fleeting glimpses of something wanly human behind the over-made-up mask of spite. This slight mellowing is typical of the dramatization as a whole. Concentrating on a narrower span than Osborne's autobiography, it weeds out its pricklier features — such as the rank snobbery and rambling abuse. . . . Where the play is at its best is in its evocation of war-time Britain. Crowds scurry, under umbrellas, to air-raid shelters as sirens wail through the drizzle; at the empty seaside — bunting flapping horizontally in a stiff breeze — grey waves splash up barbed-wire beaches or around the sandbagged pier. . . . Soaking it all in is the young Osborne — unfalteringly played as a lost-looking boy in Burbery and balaclava by Gary Capelin, and rather more awkwardly as a toffee-nosed, plummy-voiced adolescent by Neil McPherson.

Peter Kemp, 'Ending up Odd',
Times Literary Supplement, 12 July 1985

A Better Class of Person seems to me to be one of the most complex, acute and moving things that he has written. With marvellous precision, it delineates those shifting emotional allegiances which are the condition of childhood, those secret, often random loyalties woken by impulses too deep for reason and whose influence continually overshadows the person we think we have become. . . . As Osborne's father, Alan Howard was a frail, warm and dignified man emotionally stonewalled by a wife who could give him no comfort.

> Andrew Rissik, 'Cross-Fire', *New Statesman*, 12 July 1985

It went wrong because everyone who appeared was increasingly more frightful: the strange headmaster in a beret administering punishment as absently as a revolutionary tribune, the unfeeling lady almoner, the crazed matron who made bedwetters stand through breakfast, damp sheets over their heads. Cats fought. Grandmothers smelled. German fighter planes tried to kill one. Even the one young woman who listened did not hear when the boy shouted a farewell. . . . It is fatal when you start to disbelieve a writer. There were scenes that were just not explained. Why did the boarding school headmaster attack Osborne? There were others which were just irrelevant, like the one in which he goes to buy tobacco for the head with a beret. Characters appear only to trail through the fingers. But you parted company finally because *A Better Class of Person* just did not work as drama. There was no structure. The unremitting bitterness deepened and it all went nowhere.

> Byron Rogers, 'Osborne's Growing Pain', *Sunday Times*, 7 July 1985

I want to make people feel, to give them lessons in feeling. They can think afterwards. In some countries this could be a dangerous approach, but there seems little danger of people feeling too much — at least not in England as I am writing. . . . All art is organized evasion. You respond to Lear or Max Miller — or you don't. I can't teach the paralyzed to move their limbs. Shakespeare didn't describe symptoms or offer explanations. Neither did Chekhov. Neither do I. . . .

I am a writer and my own contribution to a socialist society is to demonstrate those values in my own medium, not to discover the best ways of implementing them. I don't need to step outside my own home to canvass for the Labour Party. . . . Nobody can be very interested in my contribution to a problem like the kind of houses people should have built for them, the kind of school they should send their children to, or the pensions they should be able to look forward to. But there are other questions to be asked — how do people live inside those houses? What is their relationship with one another, and with their children, with their neighbours and the people across the street, or on the floor above? What are the things that are important to them, that make them care, give them hope and anxiety? What kind of language do they use to one another? What is the meaning of the work they do? Where does the pain lie? What are their expectations? What moves them, brings them together, makes them speak out? Where is the weakness, the loneliness? Where are the things that are unrealized? Where is the strength? Experiment means asking questions, and these are all the questions of socialism.

'They Call it Cricket', *Declaration*, p. 47, 51-2, 65-6

What I would like most of all — although of course it's not something you can legislate for — is to see artists in the theatre being allowed to *play* at their work. Everything has to be so serious and specific all the time. . . . The element of *play* seems to have gone out of life, but artists should have the right to relax, to be frivolous, to indulge themselves in their work. The people who do it most obviously are painters. You can see very graphically the *play* in some of Picasso's work, handling bits of newspapers and bottles with the frivolity of a deeply serious, dedicated, marvellous artist. I think we should all be allowed that kind of scope for a complete artistic freedom, so that sometimes we don't have to please audiences or please critics or please anybody but ourselves.

'That Awful Museum' (1961), *A Casebook*, p. 65

One has to make a choice. I have a concrete job. I work with people and space and words. This is what I can do best of all, and entering that other arena of public pronouncements is debilitating and depressing.

Quoted by Polly Devlin, 'John Osborne', *Vogue*, June 1964, p. 168

We really do live in a wicked world. I believe that writers should express their position about this as well as they can and in the country in which they have elected to live. Writers are often more thoughtful than the rest of the community and occasionally more literate. However, they should speak modestly as gifted or admired individuals and not as part of a privileged pressure group with access to revealed truths.

'Intellectuals and Just Causes', *Encounter*, 29, Sept. 1967, p. 3-4

I've always had leftist, radical sympathies. On the other hand, I'm an authoritarian in many ways, simply because of the kind of work I do. If I didn't subscribe to some kind of discipline, I wouldn't be able to do it.

Quoted by Kenneth Tynan, 'Osborne',
The Observer, 7 July 1968, p. 21

5: A Select Bibliography

a. Primary Sources

The Plays

The plays are all separately published; there are as yet no collections.

Articles and Essays

'Sex and Failure', *The Observer*, 20 Jan. 1957. [On Tennessee Williams.]

'Replies to a Questionnaire', *Sight and Sound*, 26, Spring 1957, p. 180-5. [Answers seven questions around 'commitment' in the arts.]

'The Writer in his Age', *London Magazine*, 4, May 1957, p. 47-9; reprinted in *John Osborne: Look Back in Anger: a Casebook*, ed. John Russell Taylor (Macmillan, 1968). [Answers to another questionnaire on 'commitment'.]

'They Call it Cricket', *Declaration*, ed. Tom Maschler (MacGibbon and Kee, 1957), p. 61-84. [Major statement of his views at this time.]

'Introduction', *International Theatre Annual*, 2, ed. Harold Hobson (Calder, 1957), p. 9-10.

'Come on in – the Revolution Is Only Just Beginning', *Tribune*, 27 March 1959, p. 11. [Optimistic piece: Royal Court Th. is improving much of English theatre.]

'The American Theatre', *Encore*, No. 19, Mar. –Apr. 1959, p. 17-21.

'The Epistle to the Philistines', *Tribune*, 13 May 1960; reprinted in *A Casebook*. [Against monarchy in Biblical style.]

'Schoolmen of the Left', *The Observer*, 30 Oct. 1960, p. 17.

'That Awful Museum', *Twentieth Century*, 169, Feb. 1961, p. 212-16; reprinted in *A Casebook*. [Comments on influence of theatre, prospects of the National Th., etc.]

'A Letter to my Fellow Countrymen', *Tribune*, 18 Aug. 1961; reprinted in *A Casebook* and in *Voices from the Crowd*, ed. David Boulton (1964), p. 154-5. ['Damn you, England' because of drift to nuclear war.]

'This Monumental Swindle Called the Common Market', *Tribune*, 12 Oct. 1962, p. 5.

'The Pioneer at the Royal Court: George Devine', *The Observer*, 23 Jan. 1966.

'On Critics and Criticism', *Sunday Telegraph*, 28 Aug. 1966; reprinted in *A Casebook*.

'Intellectuals and Just Causes', *Encounter*, 29, Sept. 1967, p. 3-4.
[Contributes to symposium: writers should comment 'modestly' on this 'wicked world'.]

'On the Thesis Business and Seekers after the Bare Approximate', *The Times*, 14 Oct. 1967.

Letter, *The Times*, 2 Sept. 1968, p. 7. [Retracts 'Damn you, England'.]

'My Vote', *The Observer*, 6 Oct. 1974, p. 23. [Labour 'with even emptier heart than usual'.]

'My Jubilee Year', *The Observer*, 6 Feb. 1977, p. 25, 27.
[Autobiographical reflections prompted by Queen's Silver Jubilee.]

'Superman? A Look Back in Anguish' (letter), *The Guardian*, 23 June 1977, p. 12. [Attacks Bernard Shaw as 'posturing wind and rubbish'.]

'Up Jumped a Playwright' (letter), *The Guardian*, 14 July 1977, p. 12.
[Damn you, Australia, for the 'crunch of jackboots' and 'rampant homosexuality'.]

'On the Writer's Side', *At the Royal Court*, ed. Richard Findlater (Amber Lane, 1981), p. 19-26.

'Mafia Maestro' (letter), *The Listener*, 10 June 1982. [His work as a TV critic is a 'light-hearted profitable exercise'.]

'What's Wrong at the National', *Sunday Times*, 25 Sept. 1983, p. 43.
[Review of *Peter Hall's Diaries*.]

'Great Sighs of Today', *The Spectator*, 22 Dec. 1984, p. 24-5. [Attacks the language of the Anglican Church's Alternative Service Book.]

'Diary', *The Spectator*, 13 July 1985, p. 7; 20 July, p.7; 27 July, p. 7; 3 Aug., p. 7

'The Shabby End to a Theatrical Dream', *The Observer*, 6 July 1986, p. 8. [Attacks National Theatre.]

'The Diary of a Somebody', *The Spectator*, 29 Nov. 1986, p. 31-2.
[Review of *The Orton Diaries*.]

Interviews

Richard Findlater, 'The Angry Young Man', *New York Times*, 29 Sept. 1957, II, p. 1, 3.

David Dempsey, 'Most Angry Fella', *New York Times Magazine*, 20 Oct. 1957, p. 22, 25-7.

John Booth, 'Rebel Playwright', *New York Times*, 2 Nov. 1958, II, p.3.

Walter Wager, ed., *The Playwrights Speak* (New York: Dell, 1967), p. 90-109. [TV interview with John Freeman, Jan. 1962.]

Stephen Watts, 'Playwright John Osborne Looks Back — and not in Anger', *New York Times*, 22 Sept. 1963, II, p. 1.

Polly Devlin, 'John Osborne', *Vogue*, June 1964, p. 98-9, 152, 168.

Charles Hussey, 'Osborne Looks Forward in Anger', *New York Times Magazine*, 25 Oct. 1964, p. 71-2, 74, 76, 78, 81.

'John Osborne Talks to Kenneth Tynan', *The Observer*, 30 June 1968, p. 21.

'Osborne', *The Observer*, 7 July 1968, p. 21. [Continues interview with Tynan.]

Lewis Funke, *Playwrights Talk about Writing* (Chicago: Dramatic Publishing Co., 1975), p. 198-216. [Interview conducted in 1968.]

'John Osborne, in Conversation with Iain Johnstone, Takes a Black View of Film Work', *The Listener*, 3 July 1969, p. 17.

A. Alvarez, 'John Osborne and the Boys at the Ball', *New York Times*, 28 Sept. 1969, II, p. 1, 6. [*A Patriot for Me*.]

'Osborne the Romantic', *The Times*, 28 Aug. 1970, p. 6.

Anne Chisholm, 'Writing for Television is like Writing Short Stories', *Radio Times*, 17-23 Oct. 1970.

Sydney Edwards, 'Osborne, the Little Englander', *Evening Standard*, 30 July 1971.

Terry Coleman, 'Osborne without Anger', *The Guardian*, 12 Aug. 1971.

Keith Dewhurst, 'What Osborne Saw West of Suez', *Evening Standard*, 6 Dec. 1971.

'John Osborne', *Olivier*, ed. Logan Gourlay (Weidenfeld and Nicolson, 1973), p. 145-56.

Ruth Inglis, 'The Osborne's Dream Sequins', *Radio Times*, 4 Oct. 1973, p. 15.

Caryl Brahms, 'The Vein of Anger is Still There', *Guardian Weekly*, 24 Aug. 1974, p. 18.

Mark Amory, 'Jester Flees the Court', *Sunday Times Magazine*, 24 Nov. 1974, p. 34, 36.

John Osborne in Conversation with Dilys Powell (tape, British Council Literature Study Aids, 1977). [Interview in Mar. 1976.]

Robert Chesshyre, ' "Fifty is a Young Age" for an Angry Man', *The Observer*, 18 Nov. 1979, p. 52.

W.J. Weatherby, 'Middle Age of the Angry Young Men', *Sunday Times Magazine*, 1 Mar. 1981, p. 32-3.

Valerie Grove, 'A Better Class of Osborne', *New Standard*, 6 Mar. 1981.

Bryan Appleyard, 'A Stance that Never Faltered', *The Times*, 11 May 1983, p. 16.

'Stephen Pile Calls on John Osborne', *Sunday Times*, 14 Aug. 1983, p. 33.

Melvyn Bragg, 'A Line-up of One-liners', *The Observer*, 8 June 1986.

b: Secondary Sources

Full-length Studies

Martin Banham, *Osborne* ('Writers and Critics'). Oliver and Boyd,
   1969.
Alan Carter, *John Osborne*. Oliver and Boyd, revised ed., 1973.
Harold Ferrar, *John Osborne*. ('Columbia Essays on Modern Writers').
   New York: Columbia U.P., 1973. [48-page study.]
Herbert Goldstone, *Coping with Vulnerability: the Achievement of
   John Osborne*. Washington: University Presses of America, 1982.
Ronald Hayman, *John Osborne*. Heinemann Educational, revised ed.,
   1972.
Arnold Hinchliffe, *John Osborne* . Boston: Twayne, 1984.
Simon Trussler, *John Osborne*. Longmans Green for British Council,
   1969. [39-page study.]
Simon Trussler, *The Plays of John Osborne*. Gollancz, 1969.

Articles and Chapters in Books

Kenneth Allsop, *The Angry Decade* (Peter Owen, 1958), p. 96-132,
   135-40.
Michael Anderson, *Anger and Detachment* (Pitman, 1976), p. 21-49.
Arthur N. Athanason, 'John Osborne', *British Dramatists since World
   War II*, ed. Stanley Weintraub, Dictionary of Literary Biography,
   13 (Detroit: Gale Research, 1982), p. 371-92.
Michael Billington, 'The Cartoon Image is a Potential Angry Brigade
   Member', *The Guardian*, 18 Dec. 1973, p. 10.
John Russell Brown, *Theatre Language* (Allen Lane, Penguin Press,
   1972), p. 118-57.
Terry Browne, *Playwrights' Theatre: the English Stage Company at the
   Royal Court* (Pitman, 1975).
B. Denning, 'John Osborne's War against the Philistines', *Hudson
   Review*, 11, 1959, p. 411-19.
John Elsom, *Post-War British Theatre* (Routledge and Kegan Paul,
   1976), p. 72-81.
Gareth Lloyd Evans, *The Language of Modern Drama* (Dent, 1977),
   p. 102-13.
——'The Seven Lives of Jimmy Porter', *Manchester Guardian
   Weekly*, 30 June 1966, p. 13.
Steven H. Gale, 'John Osborne: Look Forward in Fear', *Essays on
   Contemporary British Drama*, ed. Hedwig Bock and Albert
   Wertheim (Munich: Max Hueber, 1981), p. 5-29.

Select Bibliography

Gabriel Gersh, 'The Theater of John Osborne', *Modern Drama*, 10, Sept. 1967, p. 137-43.

Ronald Hayman, *British Theatre since 1955* (Oxford U.P., 1979), p. 34-8.

Arnold P. Hinchliffe, *British Theatre 1950-70* (Oxford: Blackwell, 1974), p. 58-76.

——'Whatever Happened to John Osborne?', *Contemporary English Drama*, ed. C.W.E. Bigsby (Stratford-upon-Avon Studies, 19, Arnold, 1981), p. 52-63.

G.K. Hunter, 'The World of John Osborne', *Critical Quarterly*, 3, 1961, p. 76-81.

David H. Karrfalt, 'The Social Theme in Osborne's Plays', *Modern Drama*, 13, 1970, p. 78-82.

Andrew Kennedy, *Six Dramatists in Search of a Language* (Cambridge U. P., 1975), p. 192-212.

Laurence Kitchin, *Drama in the Sixties* (Faber, 1966), p. 185-91. [*Luther* and *Inadmissible Evidence*.]

John Lahr, 'Poor Johnny One-Note', *Theatre 72*, ed. Sheridan Morley (Hutchinson, 1972), p. 185-97; reprinted from *Up against the Fourth Wall* (New York: Grove Press, 1970), p. 230-45.

Charles Marowitz, *Confessions of a Counterfeit Critic* (Eyre Methuen, 1973). [*George Dillon, Plays for England, A Bond Honoured*.]

Graham Martin, 'A Look Back at Osborne', *Universities and Left Review*, No. 7, Autumn 1959, p. 37-40.

Karl Miller, 'Second Opinion, 2: John Osborne', *Sunday Times Magazine*, 20 Nov. 1966, p. 83, 86.

Benedict Nightingale, 'The Fatality of Hatred', *Encounter*, 58, May 1982, p. 63-70.

David I. Rabey, *British and Irish Political Drama in the Twentieth Century* (Macmillan, 1986), p. 78-84.

Mark Roberts, *The Tradition of Romantic Morality* (Macmillan, 1973), p. 1-26.

Ian Scott-Kilvert, 'The Hero in Search of a Dramatist', *Encounter*, 11, Dec. 1957, p. 26-30.

John Russell Taylor, *Anger and After* (Methuen, revised ed., 1969), p. 39-66; earlier version reprinted in *John Osborne: 'Look Back in Anger': a Casebook*, p. 75-100.

Irving Wardle, 'Looking Back on Osborne's Anger', *New Society*, 1 July 1965, p. 22-3.

——'Osborne and the Critics', *New Society*, 16 June 1966, p. 22-3.

——*The Theatres of George Devine* (Cape, 1978). [Background on Royal Court Th.]

Katharine J. Worth, *Revolutions in Modern English Drama* (G. Bell, 1973), p. 67-85.

Reference Sources

Kimball King, *Twenty Modern British Playwrights: a Bibliography, 1956 to 1976* (New York: Garland, 1977), p. 85-124.

Cameron Northouse and Thomas P. Walsh, *John Osborne: a Reference Guide* (Boston: G.K. Hall, 1974). [Annotated bibliography, better with American material than with British.]